Careers in the Nonprofit Sector

DOING WELL BY DOING GOOD

TERRY W. McADAM

The Taft Group ● Washington, D.C.

Library of Congress Cataloging-in-Publication Data

McAdam, Terry W.
  Careers in the nonprofit sector.

    Bibliography: p.
    1. Vocational guidance.   2. Job hunting.
3. Corporations, Nonprofit.   I. Title.
HF5381.M12   1986   650.1′4   86-23201
ISBN 0-914756-26-5

The Taft Group is the nation's leading technologically based information organization serving the needs of nonprofit organizations and institutions, providing a wide array of data and publications in fund raising, marketing, management, and communications.

TAFT Profit Thinking for Nonprofit Organizations
5130 MacArthur Boulevard, N.W.
Washington, D.C. 20016
(202) 966-7086
(800) 424-3761

Dedication

This book is dedicated with love to Wyeth McAdam, who already charts her own course wisely and will choose her own career one day soon; Marjorie McAdam, who was there at the beginning of mine; and Glenn Walker, who didn't get to finish his own.

Table of Contents

PART III. AFTER THE OFFER

LIST OF FIGURES

LIST OF TABLES

Foreword

by Brian O'Connell

There is considerable growth in job opportunities in the independent or nonprofit sector. Though employees in nonprofit organizations receive somewhat less compensation than their counterparts in government and business, the differential is no longer so great that it requires enormous sacrifice for individual and family. In addition, various surveys indicate that the challenges and satisfactions are somewhat greater in the independent sector, offsetting the pay differential. For example, an important study, "Work and Workforce Characteristics in the Nonprofit Sector," by Phillip Mirvis and Edward Hackett reported that "nonprofit jobs provide more challenge, variety, satisfaction, and intrinsic rewards than those in private enterprise or government." Their findings indicate that these rewards will attract and retain people as long as the salary differential is not more than one third what they could make in other sectors.

These factors and growing awareness of potential careers in the sector are causing more people of all ages to explore job possibilities with voluntary organizations. This new interest in the nonprofit sector is found equally among mid-career individuals and younger persons. It is also increasingly evident among persons making a career change and retirees seeking interesting work opportunities.

Beyond personal satisfactions, the contributions of philanthropic and voluntary organizations provide an important dimension to the American experience. Most of the great movements of our society have had their origins in this independent sector, for example abolition of slavery, civil rights, libraries, child labor laws, and opportunities for the handicapped.

Today, we have developed thousands of organizations to serve a vast variety of causes. In recent times, the nonprofit sector has given birth to organizations—and potential careers—devoted to the rights of women, conservation and preservation, learning disabilities, conflict resolution, Hispanic culture and rights, education on the free enterprise system, the aged, drunk driving, voter registration, the environment, native Americans, the dying, experimental theatre, international understanding, population control, neighborhood empowerment, control of nuclear power, and on and on. American citizens volunteer and contribute to an ever-increasing number of organizations that represent a wide range of needs, aspirations, and social groups.

This growth in our country's nonprofit sector has in many cases outdistanced our capacity to attract and develop the dedicated and competent staff necessary to sustain these many diverse and vital institutions. Throughout the sector, we have considerable need for staff persons dedicated to public service, and oriented and trained for maximum citizen interest and constituent involvement.

An example might illustrate the case. The Council of Jewish Federations did an analysis to try to determine why certain of their local units did so much better than the average. They assumed that the explanation would relate to the number of Jews in those communities, their per capita income, and related factors. The largest single factor, however, was found to be quality of staff and the orientation and ability of staff to work with volunteers. As a result, the Council is now devoting a larger part of its effort to staff development.

Morton Mandel, one of the key volunteers involved in the Council's appraisal and decision, has helped to apply those lessons on a much broader scale. The Mandel Center for Nonprofit Leadership at Case Western Reserve University in Cleveland, established through Mr. Mandel's generosity, is one of a growing number of programs training people—both beginning and mid-career—for the nonprofit field. Terry McAdam, the author of this book, led a small team of knowledgeable professionals to help the Mandel Center get off to a fast start in the development of its nonprofit management teaching curriculum and continues to serve on the Center's advisory committee.

The organization that I'm proud to serve, INDEPENDENT SECTOR, is addressing another obstacle to building careers in the nonprofit sector. Up to now, the various parts of the sector have been so separate that it has not been easy to provide bridges for talented people to move from museums to foundations to voluntary health associations, even though so many of the skills and attributes are comparable. INDEPENDENT SECTOR is committed both to attracting more able people into the sector and to building career ladders in public service for them. *Careers in the Nonprofit Sector* will add greatly to that effort.

Our sector is the only one of the three sectors that does not yet invest heavily in the development of future leadership. We are so scattered and so preoccupied with immediate human needs and aspirations that almost no one has the time, money, and responsibility to attend to the fundamentals of future effectiveness.

America needs to tend to its third sector, and the sector needs to be building for its next level of contribution. Basic to that growth is our ability to attract and develop staff people committed to public service and maximum citizen service and influence. Terry McAdam's book is another important step in that direction.

Preface and Acknowledgments

Welcome to the wonderful world of seeking a career. The research people confirm that more and more of us are experiencing several careers, including more than one job in each, during our working lives. You may be thinking about starting to work or making a change in the kind of work you do. This book may open a new world to you—that of the nonprofit sector.

The book will explain this nonprofit sector and talk about how organizations that don't make a profit but do carry out a number of good works not only survive in our capitalist economy but make critical contributions to its functioning. It will speak about the people who work in these organizations and what they do. And, it will help you find a job in the sector!

The book should provide you with insights into those characteristics of the nonprofit sector that should be understood fairly well before you can decide if this sector is the appropriate one in which to seek work. By understanding this sector, you, as a job seeker, can determine for yourself whether you will like, tolerate, and truly desire to be a part of the vast and fascinating nonprofit sector.

I have tried to speak with you in a personal way throughout this book. I chose this sector myself years ago after considerable thought and soul-searching. I will address the values and beliefs that appear to me to be central to working well, doing well, and securing satisfaction in the nonprofit sector. I will try to help you think through why some people choose careers in this service-oriented sector while others do not. And if you wish to rush in "where others fear to tread" I will try to help you pursue that career of "doing well by doing good" in a clear, concrete, explicit, and purposeful manner so that the odds of your being successful in a career search will be high.

Although there is a special emphasis in this book on those who seek positions in the nonprofit sector, it should also prove quite useful to those seeking work in government or private industry. For example, chapter 5, "Forty-two Action Steps for Seeking NPO Jobs" contains a number of explicit suggestions about finding work that are applicable to any sector, thus making this book useful to persons contemplating career changes within any of the three major sectors:

the nonprofit sector, the government sector, and the for-profit private sector.

You are invited to write to me (see Conclusion for address) with suggestions, telling me where the book was helpful, and where it was not, especially if you can suggest how it might be improved.

Finally, I would like to thank the people who consented to interviews for this book, and the literally hundreds of friends, colleagues, and nonprofit sector people who helped me to develop those insights I have to offer on the sector and how to find work in it. And, a special thank you to David E. Sharpe, my editor at TAFT, and to Elizabeth Shinoda with her trusty word processor, many constructive editorial suggestions, especially regarding chapter 4, plus her encouragement to finish the total effort.

Introduction

by John Naisbitt

While most people associate me with the books I have written, I enjoyed multiple careers before I became an author. Especially valuable to me were the seven years I spent working in the nonprofit sector. (Less valuable were some of my later business ventures, which also turned out to be nonprofit enterprises.) Thus, it gives me particular pleasure to introduce this excellent book on *Careers in the Nonprofit Sector: Doing Well by Doing Good* by Terry McAdam. A little of my personal history will help you understand why.

When I graduated from college in 1953, I went to work, like many in my generation, for a large corporation. I joined Kodak, which seemed to be an excellent entry point into the "Gray Flannel Suit" world of corporate success. My stay was fairly brief. My problem with Kodak was that I decided to run for political office, which deviated from the corporate norm—a pattern of deviation which continues to this day. I'll never forget being called in by my boss at Kodak and told either to get out of politics or to get out of Kodak. I started looking for new work even before I lost the election.

Unexpectedly back out on the job market, this time I wanted to find a position I cared about, where I could fully express my creative impulses—and I wanted to be paid for it. That did not seem to be an unreasonable demand for someone like me—an idealistic, politically active, 26-year-old who had been working to integrate movie houses years before the civil rights movement had formally started.

Through friends, I was introduced to the Unitarian Service Committee of Boston, an organization which was actively involved in upgrading educational and social services in Korea and India and among Navaho Indians in the United States. I jumped at an offer to join. Almost immediately, I felt at home. While I was the youngest in age, I was treated as an equal and given huge responsibilities by my senior colleagues. I found the atmosphere more collegial and more supportive than any other place I have worked in the private and government sectors. Furthermore, the Unitarian Service Committee was leveraging a tremendous amount of social change, and I had no difficulty seeing that my efforts were producing clear-cut results. The pay was not the greatest, but the job certainly was good for my mental health.

After two years, I left the Unitarian Service Committee when I was offered what seemed to be my dream job. While I had enjoyed tremendously the social activism of the Committee, my first loves were books and cerebral undertakings. I had been spending my spare time as a volunteer discussion leader for a group dedicated to reading and talking about "the great books." Thus, I could not resist when the Great Books Foundation offered me a position in 1956 as editor of publications. Once again, I was to be paid—and given a large raise, too—for doing something I would have done anyway.

The Great Books people gave me a great deal of responsibility— more than I thought I wanted—and I loved it. I was making a difference, but in a very different way than at the Unitarian Service Committee. I was publishing material that nourished the intelligence of hundreds of thousands of people around the country.

By 1958, my family had expanded, and I was attracted by more money and a unique job opportunity in the private sector. I became the first-ever Director of Information for Montgomery Ward, the retailing company that had studiously avoided the press for the previous 75 years. This foray of mine back to corporate America lasted two years. In 1960, I joined the nonprofit world as Director of Information at the National Safety Council in Chicago. Among other duties, I became the Cassandra-like figure who went on the radio before holiday weekends to predict traffic deaths.

A long-established organization with a multimillion-dollar budget, the National Safety Council more closely resembled Montgomery Ward than the Unitarian Service Committee. Although I thoroughly enjoyed my work at the Safety Council, it felt like an ordinary job to me—as opposed to the crusade in which I had engaged with the Unitarians. Thus, when the excitement and idealism of John Kennedy's New Frontier beckoned in 1963, I could not resist. I quickly moved to Washington—thus ending my nonprofit work career.

I have stayed in touch with the nonprofit sector by serving on several nonprofit boards, and I remain committed to the idea that nonprofits have a significant role to play in our society. More importantly, nonprofits have been at the heart of the movement for social change. Usually small and struggling, along the lines of the Unitarian Service Committee, such organizations have been at the heart of fundamental shifts in thinking about civil rights, the environment, women's rights, and war and peace. The activists who run such organizations are the social entrepreneurs of our time. Other nonprofits, in the education, health, and public charity fields play less controversial, but no less important parts in American society.

I am struck by the opportunity the nonprofit sector offers both to do good and to be creative. I would be the last to claim, however, that all nonprofits perform useful functions or offer a chance for entrepreneurial talents. The fact is that the nonprofit sector reflects the rest of society. Some organizations are on the cutting edge; others lag behind. At a time when our nation and the world are going through huge change, some nonprofits are doing their utmost to preserve the 19th century, while others are leading the way into the 21st.

It is obvious to me that the "megatrends" that are transforming our lives are also transforming much of the nonprofit world. I wrote about these societal trends in my book, and the following looks briefly at each trend in terms of nonprofits.

1. *From Industrial Society to Information Society.* Very few nonprofits have ever been involved in manufacturing, so they have much less stake than does the private sector in preserving the old industrial economy. Nonprofits—whether universities, think-tanks, or research labs—have long emphasized the production, processing, and distribution of information. In many ways, the rest of society is catching up with the nonprofit world's emphasis on information. Nonprofits have, in turn, much to learn from the corporate sector in terms of harnessing entrepreneurial energy, using new technologies, and developing management skills.

2. *Forced-Technology to High Tech/High Touch.* Any student who has been treated as a number on a computer printout by a large university can testify how distasteful new technology can be. Whenever new technology is introduced, there must be a countervailing human response—that is, "high touch." Consequently, there has been an upsurge in student interest in smaller, less alienating universities. Similarly, great advances in medical technology have often led to—or been accompanied by—greater personal involvement in health issues. Alternative medical treatment, the physical fitness movement, and hospices for the dying all illustrate this trend.

3. *National Economy to World Economy.* As the world economy becomes increasingly interconnected, there is growing recognition that perceptions of related problems such as poverty, hunger, and pollution also must be globalized. Obviously, Americans have long tried to solve international problems through nonprofits, such as my former employer, the Unitarian Service Committee. Yet, there is now emerging a new breed of multinational, nonprofit corporation. Such multinational nonprofits, of which the "Live-Aid" concert is the best known, reflect a global awareness based on mutual interdependence. Another such organization is Search for Common Ground, on whose

board I serve. This organization develops practical ways of moving the world away from "win-lose" thinking to "win-win" approaches in dealing with international problems.

4. *Short-Term to Long-Term.* Nonprofits have traditionally dealt with short-term crises—whether housing the homeless, feeding the starving, or healing the sick. As global problems grow, however, more must be done. It is not enough only to clean up pollution. We must consider the effects on our grandchildren and think about what kind of world we want to leave them. Nonprofits such as the Worldwatch Institute, the Institute for Contemporary Studies, and Search for Common Ground are developing plans of action on such questions.

5. *Centralization to Decentralization.* Some nonprofits, but by no means all, are tied to the grassroots. For example, as the Nuclear Freeze movement, born in local activism around the country, and the New Right, emerging out of grassroots action and funding, have both focused more and more on national and international issues, they seem determined to retain their decentralized grassroots character. Moreover, some of the larger, more centralized organizations are delegating more autonomy and control over their resources to outlying branches (of YMCA's, for example) or local units. There has always been a "keep it tied to the streets" syndrome in this sector . . . and it is finding new voice.

6. *From Institutional Help to Self-Help.* Americans are more and more weaning themselves from dependence on large institutions. In a sense, we are reclaiming our traditional sense of self-reliance after decades of trusting, perhaps a bit too much, in institutional help. Nonprofits and medical schools are reacting—albeit slowly—to growing trends toward wellness, preventive medicine, and holistic care and away from the old model of illness, drugs, surgery, and treating symptoms rather than the whole person. At the same time, new nonprofits are springing up to work within the wellness model. Fifteen million Americans now belong to some 500,000 self-help organizations. These people have formed new groups, usually nonprofit, to deal with almost every conceivable problem, including—among many more—retirement, weight control, alcohol and drug abuse, divorce, and child abuse.

7. *From Representative Democracy to Participatory Democracy.* In the nonprofit world, as elsewhere, there is a trend toward making people part of the process of arriving at decisions that affect their lives. Many universities have students and faculty on their boards. Hospitals pay more attention to patients' concerns. Political action organizations,

from Common Cause to the right-to-life groups, look increasingly to their membership in setting their agenda.

8. *From Hierarchies to Networking.* Top-down, hierarchical structures are being by-passed by nonhierarchical networks. Networks, whether among universities, consumers, or health care providers, provide a horizontal link among like-minded people or groups. Examples in the nonprofit field include the National Women's Health Network, Inc., which provides services for runaway children and their families; and the California Food Network, a grocery marketing system in San Francisco.

9. *From North to South (and East to West).* One of the main problems with nonprofits, more than with the rest of society, is that their leaders still believe New York and Washington, D.C. are important. While the bellwether states are California, Washington, Colorado, and Texas, and the ten cities of greatest opportunity are in the Southwest and West, nonprofits with national outreach still tend to be headquartered in the Northeast corridor. An exception was the national Nuclear Freeze movement, which, when it finally decided it needed a national office, chose St. Louis as the site.

10. *From Either/Or to Multiple Option.* People working in nonprofits increasingly do not have to make limiting personal choices. Women are not forced to decide between work and family. In most organizations, they can have both. Not all work is nine-to-five. Part-time, flextime, and working at home are all part of the multiple options available in many groups. Jobs once reserved for one sex or the other are now available to all.

In short, for those working in nonprofits (or thinking about it) as well as those working elsewhere in our society, and as I wrote at the end of *Megatrends*:

> We have extraordinary leverage and influence—individually, professionally and institutionally—if we can only get a clear sense, a clear conception, a clear vision of the road ahead.
> My God, what a fantastic time to be alive!

You, too, can do well by doing good! I trust you will find Terry McAdam's book very useful in taking on the future.

PART I

EXPLORING THE NONPROFIT SECTOR

THE SECTOR DEFINED

This first chapter defines and then provides the basic facts about and characteristics of the large, dynamic nonprofit sector. We can divide the American economy, like Gaul, into three parts: (1) the private, profit-making sector, (2) the government sector, including all three levels: federal, state, and local, and (3) the nonprofit, or as it is sometimes called independent or third, sector. See figure 1-1 below.

Fig. 1-1: Sectors of the American economy

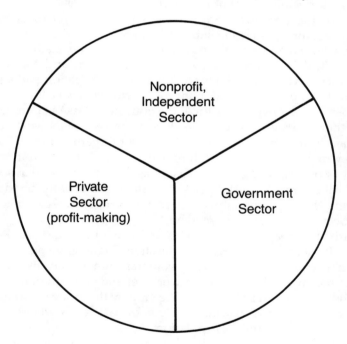

DISTINGUISHING CHARACTERISTICS

Several characteristics distinguish the nonprofit sector. First, the organizations that operate in it do not generally attempt to make a profit and retain it. Nor do they attempt to return such a profit to those persons or institutions providing the financial and human resources that help the enterprise carry out its mission. In fact, the law precludes people or institutions from profiting through investments in or contributions to nonprofit organizations (NPOs).

Second, primacy of cause is foremost to the majority of these NPOs. Said another way, the main purpose of the nonprofit organization's existence is to carry out some good work or to advocate, pursue, or advance cause. These causes run fully across the political spectrum from the far left to the far right and address thousands of issues of interest to some segment of our country's population.

Third, the nonprofit sector has deep and healthy roots in our country's history. It stems in substantial part from our rich and varied religious heritage. This religious heritage is a rope made of many strands. Buddha, Confucius, Jesus, Mohammed, and Moses "all taught that service beyond one's self is both an obligation and a joy."[1]

Fourth, the health of the nonprofit sector is viewed by many as tied closely to the overall health of the entire society. As James Douglas, author of *Why Charity* wrote during his two years as Research Associate in the Yale Program on Nonprofit Organizations, "The extent to which, in any society, Third Sector organizations are free and healthy is probably as good a measure as any of how far that society can be called free . . . . As (social) systems move toward the ideal of freedom, the separation between the government sector and the Third Sector becomes more marked."[2]

Fifth, the heart of the sector is voluntary in nature. As Robert Payton, President of the Exxon Education Foundation put it, "The irreducible core of the sector is its voluntary dimension. By organizing our society so that important work depends on voluntary action we activate the moral imagination. We employ the model of voluntary action as a means of teaching virtue: of caring for others, in its simplest and most familiar expression."[3]

Sixth, there is greater diversity and variety in the sector. The heterogeneity of purpose for the organizations in the sector is very substantial. The purposes often can contradict one another or be totally unrelated. Under the non profit sector tent, then, exist many different types of organizational camels.

Seventh, although direct service provision is the meat and potatoes of the sector, advocacy and activism are among the very impor-

4

tant functions which NPOs have in our society. They try in thousands of ways to make things better.

Finally, the sector is labor intensive. In general, its people and their services, rather than manufactured goods, are the output of the sector. This means a higher percentage of jobs per dollar of service or product produced.

THE ECONOMIC VIEW

Employment and Earnings

In economic terms, the nonprofit sector is a large one. For example, it contains a substantial share of our total economy's employment, earnings, income, and organizations. More specifically, the nonprofit sector provides:

- 9.2% of all total employment—some 10.2 million persons.[4] And the sector has experienced an upward growth trend, as summarized in table 1.
- 7.5% of total earnings from work in the United States—some $16 billion.[5] (For more on earnings, see chapter 3, "The Rewards: Compensation, Benefits, and Security.")
- 5.5% of all national income—$123 billion.[6]
- Roughly 4.4% of all organizations operating in the United States— 785,000 organizations.[7]

Table 1-1: Nonprofit sector employment

	1974	1977	1980
# of Employed (millions)	8.3M	9.3M	10.2M
% of all U.S. Employed Persons	8.3%	9.1%	9.2%

Source: Virginia A. Hodgkinson and Muray S. Weitzman, Dimensions of the Independent Sector; A Statistical Profile Washington, D.C., Independent Sector 1984.

As you can see, nonprofit organizations are an important and constructive economic force in our society. They contribute significantly to the economy, spending each year for goods and services more than $800 per person for every man, woman, and child in the United States.

This sector is also quite dynamic. Lester Salamon of the Urban Institute and his team studied some sixteen communities across our country. Their analysis revealed that two-thirds of the organizations in the nonprofit sector had been created since 1960.[8] There is no evidence of which I am aware to suggest that the birthrate of new institutions has declined. Moreover, in looking at a sample of the largest NPOs, one is immediately struck by the contradiction of seeing *both* the very familiar organization and some never heard of before (see appendix A for a list of some of the largest nonprofit organizations).

Government Support

The nonprofit sector also is involved in an intimate, if not some-times tenuous, relationship with the government sector. For example, Lester Salamon has identified five major characteristics of the existing government support of nonprofit organizations:

1. *It is extensive.* Dr. Salamon and his group estimate that $40.3 billion was provided to the sector from the federal government in 1980 with an additional $8-10 billion in state and local government funds.
2. *It is concentrated on particular subsegments.* For example, over 60 percent of 1980 government support to the nonprofit sector went to hospitals and other NPO health providers.
3. *It is far more dominant in some kinds of organizations than others.* Federal support ranges from an average of 55 percent in social service organizations down to 0 percent in religious congregations. Religious groups, however, provide social services of many different types, some of which receive government support. Note that some organizations have come close to complete dependency on government funds.
4. *It takes many forms.* These range from cash grants to purchase of service agreements and can go directly or via organizational or individual intermediaries.
5. *It varies among geographical areas.* The East and Midwest make the heaviest use of private and nonprofit organizations to provide various services, whereas the West, and especially the South, rely more heavily on public institutions.[9]

Not only has government provided substantial support for the nonprofit sector, but it has also stimulated it to grow and expand. It has increased the scale and scope of the nonprofit sector in many different ways—by, for example, stimulating it to take on many new tasks in education, health care delivery and the arts to name just a few.

ORGANIZATIONAL VIEWS

The nonprofit sector is large, and touches in some way each of our lives. Because of its far-reaching impact, the sector is viewed in different ways by various segments of our society. How you view it depends on your vantage point.

"Hard" and "Soft" NPOs

Author and nonprofit sector expert Waldemar Nielsen draws a distinction between "hard" and "soft" NPOs. "Cultural centers, colleges, hospitals, churches, and research laboratories, constitute the established, highly structured 'hard' portion of the Third Sector. The 'soft' part, though it lacks such institutional crust, is equally large and in its fashion equally significant. It consists of that great amorphous body of groups and associations devoted to causes and to change—civil rights, environmental protection, women's liberation, . . . and tens of thousands of others—collectively called the social action movements."[10]

Mr. Nielsen has identified a series of distinctions between these "hard" and "soft" elements of the nonprofit sector that are relevant to the potential job seeker. He identified the "hard" NPOs as:

- "generally older, larger, better housed, professionally staffed, and better financed."
- "concerned primarily with the provision of services."
- focused upon "specialized functions—education, care of the ill, research, assistance to the needy, the performance of religious rites, and the presentation of artistic events."[11]

"The social action movements are less structured, dependent largely on volunteer staff, minimally funded, and sometimes temporary in existence."[12]

It is important to understand that the distinctions made above are more explicit and "true" at the conceptual level than in practice. The individual organizations can be catalogued along different points in the continuum from "hard" to "soft"—as they develop over time. But, the distinctions are useful in helping you to think about the different elements of the nonprofit sector.

The Sector by Service Area

The sector, while appearing amorphously large in concept, is not amorphous in practice. When viewed by areas of service, it clearly contains many distinct parts as illustrated by figure 1-2 below.

Fig. 1-2: Sample segments of the nonprofit sector

These separate parts are differentially developed in terms of their financial, managerial, technological, and programmatic characteristics. See figure 1-3 below.

Fig. 1-3: The differential development of the nonprofit sector's segments

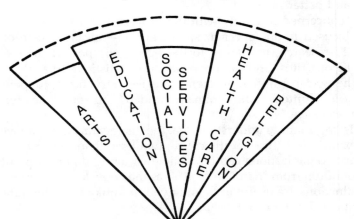

Note: The broken line of the circle's outer rim represents optimum development along any number of characteristics. Naturally, individual organizations within each subsegment will vary significantly in terms of their development. In addition, other organizational features such as size (small to large) and approach to issues (ranging from proactive to reactive) vary considerably.

The Sector by Type of Organization

Another way to look at nonprofit sector organizations is via a rough taxonomy developed by Dr. Michael O'Neill, the Director of an excellent master's level training program on nonprofit organization management at the University of San Francisco, California. A summary of Dr. O'Neill's taxonomy, in which he divides the sector into eleven groupings, is provided below.

1. *Religious organizations.* These serve the roughly 90 percent of Americans who believe in God and the 60 percent who are members of some church, synagogue, or other organized form of worship. Religious organizations are particularly important in our country, receiving roughly one-half of the money contributed to the sector from all sources.

2. *Private nonprofit educational organizations.* These organizations serve nearly 4 million students at the elementary and secondary school levels, some 9 percent of the total school population. Dr. O'Neill reports that roughly 90 percent of these students are in church-related schools. Another 2.7 million students are in private nonprofit postsecondary institutions, a little less than one-quarter of total enrollment, down from about one-half of total enrollment in the 1950s. From a job seeker's viewpoint, take note of two points: (1) the shift from private nonprofit to public universities and (2) the fact that many positions may well be quite similar in the public as compared with private nonprofit universities.

3. *Arts, cultural, historical, and community-educational organizations.* A little over one-half of the country's some 4,500 museums are private nonprofit. In addition, there are 1,500 symphony orchestras, 1,000 opera companies, and thousands of nonprofit theaters. Finally, there are tens of thousands of smaller arts, cultural, historical, communications, and other community-educational organizations.

4. *Health service organizations.* One of the giant segments of the nonprofit sector, health care, accounts for nearly one-half of

9

the employment, operating expenditures, and physical and financial assets of the nonprofit sector. For example, the sector includes some 3,500 hospitals with 700,000 beds plus 2,300 nonprofit nursing facilities and roughly 5,000 other outpatient care and allied health care services organizations.

5. *Human and social service organizations.* This segment contains the largest number of nonprofit organizations by far, with Dr. O'Neill's estimates covering a range of from 300,000 to as many as 5 million depending on how one counts institutional noses.

6. *Scientific research organizations.* Meaningful estimates are very difficult for this group since they are so intertwined with academic organizations, both public and private nonprofit. Suffice it to say that there are a number of them (in the low thousands, I would estimate) geographically disbursed, and extremely labor intensive.

7. *Business, professional, farming, and labor organizations.* Many of these organizations, although exempt from corporate income tax, may not receive tax-deductible donations. Many of them are more oriented in conceptual terms to the private for-profit sector—but they do qualify as nonprofit organizations.

8. *Mutual benefit organizations.* Employing over 300,000 employees, a number of these organizations have played crucial roles in helping immigrants adjust and survive or in assisting victims of particular diseases cope with life.

9. *Community development organizations.* These organizations are highly disbursed geographically but generally have small and somewhat specialized staffs. Their main focus is job development, economic development, housing, and possibly work on the capital infrastructure of the locality.

10. *Legislative, legal, political, and advocacy organizations.* These organizations, although fairly small in number and employment, are often engaged in the most current, visible, and dramatic issues affecting the sector. For example, these organizations include such groups as: Common Cause, the National Organization of Women, the Sierra Club, the Urban League, the NAACP, the National Coalition Against Domestic Violence, the Heritage Foundation, and organizations in the disarmament and peace movement. They cover all elements of the political and social spectrum. And, more important, contribute heavily to the vibrance, vigor, and diversity of our society.

11. *Grantmaking organizations.* It is important to remember that foundations and corporations are a small part of philanthropy, representing 6 percent and 5 percent of total giving respectively, whereas individuals accounted for 89 percent, according to the 1984 American Association of Fund-Raising Counsel figures.

As a foundation executive, I cannot resist the temptation to elaborate on this last grouping. Although there are some 30,000 foundations registered, only about 3,500 are of any significant size. Rough surveys by the Council on Foundations indicate there are only one to two thousand full-time jobs in foundations with another three to four thousand part-time jobs added on. The bulk of the jobs are in New York City, with Boston, Chicago, Minneapolis, Los Angeles, and San Francisco as the other major centers.

Most of the jobs are within small organizations containing two to three full-time professionals. If you seek a medium or large organization, with substantial upward mobility, this subsegment of the nonprofit sector isn't for you! If it does appeal, the heart of the work involves:

- Reading proposals
- Visiting with prospective grantees
- Making judgments about the most viable or appropriate grants to make
- Writing detailed memoranda for one's board and files
- Answering questions from prospective grantees.

Many of the analytic and decision-making skills are "soft" in grantmaking. Qualitative judgments play a strong role. There is also a very heavy emphasis on writing clearly and quickly. Listening skills are vital and high levels of empathy most useful.

The advantages of work in grantmaking include substantial variety in one's work. And, it is often highly educational. By and large, the work and the positions are fairly secure and stable—but there is also limited mobility. Adding to the disadvantages are the distance from the actual service delivery, the difficulty in establishing a measurable track record, modest pay (for the most part), and heavy amounts of paper work.

Foundations also have many critics. From the legions of disappointed applicants for limited funds all too often comes the story of unanswered mail or phone calls. And, some foundations have much further to go in terms of satisfactory explanations of their program priorities to the public, or of being accountable to the public by providing at least minimal information about the nature, process, and specifics of their decisions.

Moreover, some observers of the foundation scene have been very critical of foundation leadership in defining complete problems, finding and assessing alternative solutions, and contributing to the formulation and implementation of solutions. For example, Waldemar Nielsen minced few words in his criticism of foundation leadership in his recent book, *The Endangered Sector,* when he said, "But the present generation of American foundation heads has on the whole been a dull and undistinguished lot, which has deprived the Third Sector of a much needed and formerly available stimulus."[13] I see this situation changing steadily for the better, but as a foundation executive I have a bias towards optimism about my own field. Mr. Nielsen's most recent book (*The Golden Donors*) also suggests progress is being made, though he still sees much room for improvement remaining.

NPOs as Defined by Regulation

From an official regulatory point of view, there are many different types of nonprofit organizations. The main types in which there are likely to be work are identified at right in table 1-2 by some wonderful alphabet soup and numerical combinations.

FUNCTIONS OF NPOS

The sector is not only fragmented into its major segments such as arts and culture, education, health, social services, and others as illustrated in figure 1-2; it is also fragmented into a variety of different, simple, and familiar but very important functions. The sector's people and the organizations in which they work (for pay or the joy of giving and participating) perform the following types of functions including, for example:

- Educating
- Curing
- Searching for new knowledge
- Entertaining
- Preaching, consoling and nurturing the spirit
- Lobbying for reform
- Serving and helping.

**Table 1-2. Selected types of organizations exempt
from federal income tax**

Tax	Code	No.	Type of Organization	Number of Organizations (in 1982)
501	(c)	(3)	Religious, educational, charitable, scientific, literary organizations, etc.	322,826
501	(c)	(4)	Civic leagues, social welfare organizations, local associations of employees.	131,578
501	(cc)	(5)	Labor, agricultural, horticultural organizations	86,322
501	(cc)	(6)	Business leagues, chambers of commerce, real estate boards	51,065
501	(cc)	(7)	Social and recreational clubs	54,036
501	(c)	(8)	Fraternal beneficiary societies and associations	116,549
ALL OTHER (16 remaining 501(c) designations)				79,064
TOTAL ALL TYPES				841,440

Source: U.S. Department of the Treasury, Internal Revenue Service, Exempt Organization's Master File, as cited in Michael O'Neill, Introduction to Independent Sector, Instructors Manual, University of San Francisco, Appendix B.

ROLES OF NPOS IN SOCIETY

After exploring the various ways to "slice up" or define this sector, it is useful to examine the wide variety of interesting roles[14] organizations in this sector play. These include functioning as . . .

. . . *incubators of ideas* ranging all the way from basic inventions created in the think tanks and research and development organizations such as the RAND Corporation, Santa Monica, California, to the development of major public policy initiatives in areas such as auto safety by Ralph Nader's Center for Auto Safety or the National Coalition Against Domestic Violence in the area of physical abuse of women and children.

. . . *mediating and corrective forces* addressing social problems at every level ranging from global peace on the part of the Quakers, the National Center for Defense Information in Washington, D.C., or the small but vibrant Nuclear Age Peace Foundation in Santa Barbara, CA, to state problems such as California Common Cause to the local Lion's Club, the Girl Scouts, or a Brownie troop. Many nonprofit organizations help to weave or repair the social fabric of their communities. They help people cope with the more pressing problems of life, find their version of a superior being, live through grief such as the loss of a child, or help their spirits soar through music, dance, drama, or religion. For others, they facilitate the elegance of a private thought put on a page and shared with a reading public to help those readers see and appreciate the world in a different way, confront a perplexing problem, or spend an interesting afternoon exploring the fantasy of travel through print or film.

. . . *vehicles of social integration* for the historical wave of immigrants who built this country. They also help to integrate new waves of immigrants and political refugees who continue to add to the ethnic diversity and richness of our country.

. . . *activists, catalysts, and agents* for generally constructive social change. Nonprofit organizations help us to define problems, confront them, and stimulate action on them, whether it be Mothers Against Drunk Drivers (MADD) lobbying for a more aggressive approach to preventing drunken persons from slaughtering our citizenry on the highway to efforts in hundreds of localities and states to reform the way in which public schools are operated. Such organizations provide some of the primary means by which certain persons or groups of persons can overcome the barriers and escape the confines of com-

14

partments that limit and oppress their personal fulfillment, lives, and opportunity.

. . . *direct providers of services.* Lest we think that everything in this sector is about some form of social change, many of the organizations act as implementors and direct providers of a wide variety of services financed privately, publicly, or both. The sector's advantage is that it contains many relatively smaller organizations that are closer to the point of service delivery and much more likely to attempt to be responsive to changes in the needs of our nation's people. Smaller can be better in this line of work, and in the nonprofit sector many of the smaller organizations do their best to stay in touch with our society's needs at the "street level."

Lester Salamon and his team at the Urban Institute's Nonprofit Sector Project have helped us better understand the substantial role played by NPOs in the delivery of services as "a part of a broader pattern of government action in this country . . . termed "third-party government."[15] They are referring to the use of nongovernmental nonprofit organizations to carry out federal government purposes— but with considerable discretion over the expenditure of federal funds.

. . . *safe havens for developing of and experimenting with new modes of living and human relations.* These forms of living range from the avant-garde to the counter culture and from born-again Christian approaches to human potential movements.

. . . *instrumentalities of cultural continuity* through the activities of historical societies, ethnic, and religious organizations (e.g., Ukrainian or Chinese Saturday Schools). Such institutions can also represent the sacred and the spiritual while preserving old forms of worship and enabling new forms of bonding, self-help, and spirituality.

. . . *wellsprings from which new or rediscovered ethical standards might flow.* In addition, they provide a process for measuring institutional as well as individual performance from an ethical point of view. This "well" also nurtures the development and retention of many of our social values through its institutions themselves and the process of our citizenry participating in these institutions' work, administration, and management.

. . . *sources and havens from which periodic bursts of reformism in public life can come,* including organizations which expose corruption or propose alternative means of self goverance procedures such as low income housing cooperatives.

. . . *living laboratories, in which to nurture and carry out esthetic, spiritual, and intellectual innovation.*

. . . *channels through which the impulse to altruism can be preserved, empowered, and kept alive,* ranging from the local church or synagogue to limitless local support groups for one cause or another.

. . . *some of the key pacesetters or standard improvers, for social standards in our culture and their improvement.*

Finally, it is important to know that the boundaries distinguishing the sector from the private or government sectors are fuzzy at best. As John Simon, the Director of Yale's Program on Nonprofit Organizations, has put it, the sector is like "a seamless web" with the edges very unclear. Although the edges are unclear, the heart of the sector—a concern for others expressed in a myriad of ways—has a regular and strong beat!

NOTES
Chapter 1

1. Brian O'Connell, *America's Voluntary Spirit* (New York; The Foundation Center, 1983), 1.

2. James D. Douglas, *Why Charity? The Case for a Third Sector* (Beverly Hills, Calif.: Sage Publications, 1983), 15.

3. Robert L. Payton, *Major Challenges to Philanthropy*, as quoted in Michael R. Ostrowski, "The Third Sector: From Definition to Purpose and Policy" (Paper prepared for University of Colorado at Denver doctoral program, 3 July 1985).

4. Virginia A. Hodgkinson and Murray S. Weitzman, *Dimensions of the Independent Sector: A Statistical Profile* (Washington, D.C.: Independent Sector, 1984), 1.

5. Hodgkinson and Weitzman, *Dimensions*, 10.

6. Ibid.

7. Hodgkinson and Weitzman, *Dimensions*, 15.

8. Lester M. Salamon, "The Invisible Partnership, Government and the Nonprofit Sector," *Bell Atlantic Quarterly* 1 (Autumn 1984):

9. For further examination of this information, see Lester M. Salamon, "Nonprofit Organizations and the Rise of Third-Party Government: The Scope, Character, and Consequences of Government Support of Nonprofit Organizations" (Research paper presented at Independent Sector Research Forum, 3 May, 1983).

10. Waldemar A. Nielson, *The Endangered Sector* (New York: Columbia University Press, 1979), 155.

11. Ibid.

12. Ibid.

13. Nielsen, *Endangered Sector*, 207.

14. Several of the roles for the sector discussed were adapted from Nielson, *The Endangered Sector*, 4-5.

15. Salamon, "Nonprofit Organizations," 24.

Chapter 2

THE VALUES HELD IN THE SECTOR

This chapter discusses values in the sector from the individual's point of view. It presents a melding of the key reasons people seem to choose to work in this sector and the values they see as implicit (and in some cases explicit) to working in the nonprofit sector. I have distilled these key points about why people seem to choose the sector and the values that seem to undergird their choices to help you think about whether some of these values appeal in particular to you as you think about work. But do not assume that the nonprofit sector has uniformly higher/better values or that wonderful values cannot be found in the other two sectors. To the contrary, they can!

The research underpinning this chapter is episodic. I simply have asked people "why" over the years as I have interviewed, talked with, and worked with hundreds of men and women devoted to some aspect of the nonprofit sector. *So much for the caveats.*

WHY WOULD ANYONE WANT TO WORK HERE?

The task of exploring the values in the sectors is easier because the NPO's mission has a very large influence on organizational values. "The mission of the organizations (to cure, to educate, to entertain) permeates the sector's culture and identity. It serves as both a selector and a socializer, attracting particular segments of the work force and motivating and satisfying them with particular rewards."[1] On the other hand, the task is complicated because the sector contains organizations of such diversity in size, approach, philosophy, and style. This sector does indeed follow Chairman Mao's dictum to "let a hundred flowers bloom."

More Than Just A Job

People correctly perceive work in this sector as having a particular high degree of *involvement*. Dr. Srully Blotnick uses the term "satisfying absorption" to describe this involvement.[2] More than in any other sector, people here can act and work on their values and beliefs.

Many of the people who work in the sector, whether they push papers or brooms or handle trash or scalpels, feel that their work (and, equally important, the organization or movement of which they are a part) has fairly high social relevance. They feel that what they do matters—and matters to a lot to people. The majority of the people in the sector are moving toward the goal of "making a difference." For these people, the marketplace of the private sector may not allow as much diversity and government may not be quite as hospitable to experimentation. If creative involvement is your desire, the nonprofit sector deserves a careful look.

This involvement is critically important to many people. In a study of the careers of five thousand Americans over age twenty-five, Dr. Blotnick confirmed that, especially for college-educated workers, more is wanted than just a decent wage and work that isn't too boring. These people "aren't seeking just a job; they want a career, a personally fulfilling profession. That is one goal which means quite a bit to them, more in fact than they imagine . . . . This is one work-related crisis that has a powerful, hidden effect on their personal lives."[3]

I believe it is these feelings and drives that may well be at the core of what motivates many of us to work in this sector. As Robert Payton puts it, "Voluntary participation, however, must be more than a reflex action, more than a once-a-year initialing of the payroll deduction forms; voluntary action must engage us personally and directly if it is to shape our values and beliefs and principles."[4] This desire to give time to help others is prevalent throughout our society. A 1982 Gallup Organization Survey found that 55 percent of all American adults volunteered in 1982, two-thirds for more than two hours per week.

Many individuals want a sense of helping others, especially those who are disadvantaged or need some form of helping hand. In fact, a number of segments within the nonprofit sector are sufficiently oriented toward helping others that they are often called the *helping professions* (e.g., health care delivery and social services, to name just two). And this neighborliness is widespread. It affects most of the people in the sector in terms of their attitudes and values. But it shouldn't be confused with fuzzy thinking about purpose. As Brian O'Connell, President of the Independent Sector (the umbrella group that reaches the furthest across the sector) and author of the foreword to this book, recently said in his newsletter, "We are rather proud to

20

be known as soft hearted, but rather angered to be treated as soft headed."[5]

Freedom of Action

A critical value to many people who choose to work in the sector is an above-average level of independence of action or freedom to develop one's own approaches to problems. Perhaps, because many people who choose to work in this sector are self-motivated and are personally committed to working on "the" issue or serving a particular constituency, supervisors or boards of directors feel less of a need to follow up all the time or "run the dogs with a short leash."

Related to this freedom is the personal prestige in a number of nonprofit jobs. Many nonprofit organizations are highly regarded and valued in their communities for the work that they do. People who carry out this work are often accorded a portion of this respect and community value.

A Caring Workplace

The nonprofit sector is also known as a place where just a small touch more kindness in relations between workers reigns. As a *Los Angeles Times* op-ed writer recently said, "the hurts that human beings inflict on one another at work are as real and as painful as a back injury suffered from lifting heavy machinery."[6] There seems to be less on-the-job combat in this sector and a slightly higher belief in the dignity and worth of the individual.

There is an above-average sense of fair play. People who work in the sector seem to want, in general, to give the other person the benefit of the doubt, at least the first few times. Organizational hardball seems to be played at least a little less often or vigorously.

There appears to be less pressure to "succeed" and a little less "cutthroat" competition than one finds in some private sector industries. Though in my experience and informal interviews, I have known, hired, worked with, and identified many extremely hardworking, almost driven individuals seeking to accomplish with excellence whatever they are doing. Perhaps this "a little less pressure" point comes across in this form: There seems to more live and let live in the workplace. Yet there are plenty of highly committed individuals working very hard for the welfare of others. And the most committed ones feel deeply the tension and frustration of trying to tackle complex and resistant social problems with limited tools and resources.

As the wellness craze spreads to the workplace, it hasn't necessarily begun to address mental health issues. "Pretty sweatsuits and
running shoes will not cure the blows to your self-esteem administered by an insensitive office mate. A high-fiber diet is no antidote to
what you have to swallow from a boss who divides the world into two
classes: masters and slaves. Weightlifting won't lift the weight from
your heart that comes from a monotonous, stifling job where loyalty is
not rewarded and opportunities for advancement are nil. All the
aerobics in the world will not compensate for a workplace where your
feelings are disregarded, your efforts unappreciated and your needs
for friendship unrealized."[7] However, given the sector's limited resources and the enormity of some of the social problems being tack-
led, there are times when people in the sector develop a bit of a siege
mentality. This builds very strong bonds between people inside individual organizations but hinders fresh ideas from the outside.

In this sector in particular people do seem to care about one
another. Former First Lady Rosalynn Carter said it well in a recent
speech: " . . . people really care about each other. Even in the most
devastating of circumstances, people demonstrate again and again,
that something in a human life motivates unselfish giving to others.
People show incredible creativity and great persistence in finding
ways to help one another."[8] In that same speech Mrs. Carter went on
to quote a statement sent to her by John D. Rockefeller on the day he
died. "At the heart of the third sector is individual initiative and
caring. Caring, that's the key. Caring for one another, caring for our
communities, caring for our nation."[9]

The Rewards and Their Tradeoffs

There is a sense at least in some quarters of the sector that some
nonprofit sector people are willing to accept slightly lower cash compensation in return for one or more of the following:

- higher "psychic" income: feeling good about what they do and
  its relevance to society's overall health;
- a more casual working atmosphere;
- less formal or dressy work attire;
- relatively greater benefits and fringes in some areas, such as
  more vacation, shorter work day or week, and more flexibility
  in structuring work hours;
- less "up or out" mentality vis-à-vis career ladders or tracks;
- a more humanistic, people-oriented approach to personnel
  management and greater concern for the whole person.

There are also a number of people who have successfully carved out satisfying careers in this nonprofit sector at very respectable salary levels by the standards of any of the sectors. Also, as the demand for talented people increases in the nonprofit sector, the gaps between sectors in compensation are falling to at least some degree.

IS IT FOR YOU?

It's tough to reach a simple conclusion about whether this sector is right for you. A great deal depends on the specific opportunity. But, before you decide, be aware that there are also some less attractive values and behaviors within the sector including:

- Being unwilling to share information or approaches to solving problems between organizations. This is not terribly widespread but it does happen.
- Losing sight of the basic client group for which the organization was originally established—this can happen most easily when the financial "going" gets a little rough.
- Contracting the disease of arrogance and/or a "holier than thou" attitude which seems still incurable in a few quarters and can emerge at any point in one's career unless precautions are taken.

It is very important to avoid falling into the trap of over generalizing or stereotyping this sector. The discussions and statements above have many, many exceptions. The only purpose in even identifying the topics is to sandpaper your job assessment "fingertips" so you can be sensitive to the values and workplace mores in places where you are planning to explore the possibility of work.

One useful tool for helping you think about the values as well as the people skills and attitudes in the nonprofit sector is to have some fun with appendix B, a self-test for compatibility with the nonprofit sector. If you will take some time making some notes in this appendix about how you feel regarding the factors listed there, it can give you one very useful way to begin thinking about the likelihood that you would enjoy working in the sector.

* * *

Perhaps of greatest importance about the prevailing values in this sector is that people *care*. They seem to care about others: clients, colleagues, and society at large. This has been a short chapter be-

23

cause, in many ways, the values of this sector will best be understood by digging into the rest of the book—they emerge from the remaining aspects of work in the sector. Moreover, since this sector already accommodates a wide range of values—and as you clarify your own—you can be fairly comfortable that you will be able to find a hospitable "home" for your views.

NOTES
Chapter 2

1. Philip H. Miruis and Edward J. Hackett, "Workforce and Workforce Characteristics in the Nonprofit Sector," *Monthly Labor Review* (April 1983): 3.

2. Srully Blotnick, *The Corporate Steeplechase, Predictable Crises in a Business Career* (New York: Facts on File Publications, 1984), 39.

3. Ibid., 35.

4. Payton, *Major Challenges*, 6.

5. Brian O'Connell, "Memo to Members" (Washington, D.C.: Independent Sector, 12 July 1985), 1.

6. Gloria Kottick, "Getting Rid of the *Real* Pain in the Neck," *Los Angeles Times*, 19 August 1985, pt. II, p. 5.

7. Ibid.

8. Rosalynn Carter (Speech delivered at Independent Sector Annual Meeting, New Orleans, La., October 1985).

9. Ibid.

Chapter 3

THE NATURE OF WORK IN THE SECTOR

Understanding the nature of work in the nonprofit sector at the individual level can help you, the reader, understand: (1) some of the requirements for working in the sector including the education, job skills and experience necessary to acquire these jobs; (2) the special characteristics of work in the sector including a variety of ways in which I will give you a sense of what the actual work "feels like" and (3) the likely rewards which are likely to be available to you.

THE REQUIREMENTS

All work has certain requirements that an employer will want you to meet and demands to which you, as an employee, may need to accommodate. This section explores those areas.

Education

The diversity of the sector permits entry of workers into it with the most varied and wide-ranging levels of formal educational attainment of all three sectors. There are few substantial education barriers to entry except for positions filled by persons from some of the more formal professions such law and medicine. For example, in my own field of foundation management I have hired people with very diverse academic backgrounds. This relatively greater openness and acceptance of diverse academic (and cultural) backgrounds is one important characteristic that I believe distinguishes the nonprofit sector from the other two.

For those still willing or able to contemplate the extent and nature of their academic background, it will first be necessary for you to give some serious thought to which segment of the nonprofit sector you wish to explore for work. The academic training one might take for the arts may be, at least in part, different from that which is offered for health care management or service delivery, for example. However, the more one pursues a highly focused management or administration career, the less differences are likely to occur in the educational requirements. If nonprofit management/administration is your "thing," you may want to explore the burgeoning nonprofit management training now being offered at an increasing number of schools of public administration, business, social work, and several other disciplines. (Independent Sector has recently published a guide to such programs; see appendix C for more information on it and other educational opportunities.)

If you have selected a segment of the sector with well-defined disciplines, such as health care delivery, your task of exploring further education and training is less difficult. Most of the graduate schools in such disciplines have counseling or academic advisement sections available to prospective students. And, do not overlook opportunities to gain hands-on experience through volunteer assignments, internships or, apprenticeships. A large proportion of the people interviewed as background research for this book indicated that early volunteer experience had either prepared them for their subsequent paid employment, led to their paid job, or both. You will not know if such volunteer positions are available unless you get out there and ask.

Finally, whether you seek additional formal academic training and whatever segment of the sector appeals to you, it will be extremely useful for you to expand your experience and skills in clear, concise writing and effective oral communication. Writing and public speaking courses and practicing opportunities abound in social settings, church groups, and many others. You should also learn to prepare and interpret clear financial statements and other simple quantitative documents. A standard or special nonprofit accounting course will take you a long way. And, most important, expand your capacity to motivate, train, guide, and supervise others in complex and uncertain environments. Try some human resource management courses and manage volunteers for your church or synagogue, a social group, a youth group, or a recreational club.

Never stop being a scholar of one kind or another.

Job Skills Used

To save you hunting in research libraries for other books on the nature of work in the nonprofit sector, I have provided one approach to thinking about it below. This approach addresses the basic skills needed to do the major types of work in the sector. These basic skills are organized around three groups, depending on whether the work is done with: (1) data, (2) people, or (3) things. All three catagories are important to the nonprofit sector, especially people and data. In figure 3-1

**Fig. 3-1: A hierarchy of job skills for the nonprofit sector
(grouped into work with data, people, and things)**

DATA

- Synthesizing skills, used in such tasks as creating reports, analyses, speeches, press releases, program and budget recommendations, etc., from a base of information.
- Coordinating and innovating skills, used in gathering and disseminating data, streamlining service delivery procedures, for example.
- Analytical skills, used to analyze program results, operational facts and statistics to identify ways to increase your agency's efficiency and get "biggest bang for the buck," to evaluate employee performance during job reviews, and to evaluate budgeting procedures and spending habits of your nonprofit organization.
- Compiling and computing skills, used, for example, to gather facts and statistics to track budget expenditures, to enumerate program results, and to research the needs of your community or population group to be served and the best sources of and opportunities for funding.
- Copying skills, used to disseminate information to your staff, the press, your members and constituents.
- Comparative skills, used in such tasks as comparing grant applications, proposals for program offerings to your members or constituents, service statistics, and financial reports, etc.

PEOPLE

- Mentoring skills, used to help others in such tasks as career advice, organization start-ups, and technical assistance.
- Negotiating skills, used in such tasks as hiring employees, arranging for program funding, and setting-up joint ventures between nonprofit and profit organizations.
- Instructing skills, used to manage others effectively and make task objectives clear or to educate and train others in such varied positions as a nonprofit-agency executive, cultural institution guide or docent, or nonprofit-organization board member.
- Supervisory skills, used in overseeing the activities of others to carry out the tasks set forth in such activities as obtaining grant

Fig. 3-1: A hierarchy of job skills for the nonprofit sector (con't)

funding, operating a service program, or setting up a fund-raising or media event.

- Diverting and persuading skills, used to direct others to accomplish the goals set forth, such as obtaining a favorable response to your grant proposal or application.
- Speaking skills, used in such activities as advocating your cause before organization members and potential members, the press, or the general public, or presenting a strategic plan for the year to your staff.
- Helping and serving skills, used to do something for others in such activities as following agency procedures, facilitating meetings, and carrying out support functions in such positions as secretary, budget analyst, or information booth person for an art museum.

THINGS

- Setting-up skills, used to set up or create museum displays, convention exhibits, and the like.
- Precision-working skills, used to operate machines or tools that require great care and dexterity such as design or drafting instruments in the positions of direct mail designer or art production manager, or surgical instruments or measuring devices some health care providers or medical researchers use.
- Operating-controlling skills, used to operate and maintain equipment to make it do what you want it to, from starting it up to shutting it down to keeping it going while you are using it; used in such positions as word processor operator, computer operator, and so forth.
- Driving-operating skills, used to operate vehicles in such positions as Meals-on-Wheels driver or bus operator for a transportation service for the elderly.
- Manipulating skills, used to operate machines or tools such as typewriters, telephones, or computers in such positions as typist, receptionist, telemarketer, or executive.
- Tending skills, used to monitor machine operations in such positions as computer database administrator or technician or museum gallery security guard.

Fig. 3-1: A hierarchy of job skills for the nonprofit sector (con't)

- Feeding and offloading skills, used in such tasks as emptying or filling letter sorters, keeping a ready supply of publications or forms available, or, in the case of a nonprofit zoo or aquarium, feeding and caring for animals.
- Handling skills, used to handle objects in such positions as mailroom clerk to accomplish such tasks as delivering staff mail or fulfilling member orders or requests.

---

a variety of job skills are arranged by category with the most difficult or complex at the top and the less complex skills at the bottom within each category. The list has been compiled with examples specific to the nonprofit sector and is meant to be illustrative, not inclusive of all skills.

This hierarchical approach to thinking about job skills has been popularized by Richard Bolles, director of the National Career Development Project and author of *What Color is Your Parachute: A Practical Manual for Job Hunters and Career Changers*. Job skills are explored in detail in that book, and the hierarchy is based on the *Dictionary of Occupational Titles*, U.S. Government Printing Office, Washington, D.C., 1977, modified by Dr. Sidney A. Fine.[1]

Thinking clearly and realistically about your current skills and those you would like to be able to emphasize in your future work is a critical task. Take the time at this point to get your thinking clear about what you like to do and feel comfortable doing. We all spend so much of our waking hours at our work; why not enjoy it? If you feel you need some assistance in working through which skills speak most to you, review chapter 5 in Richard Bolles' *Parachute*.

Job Titles Used

Because many nonprofit organizations serve very specific causes, you may find the number of titles with unique meanings to be slightly higher in this sector; for example, "development" has a different nonprofit context (fund raising) than its corporate, for-profit context (product development and research). Figure 3-2 is a list of definitions of job positions prepared by the Council of Foundations. Although specific for foundations (generally grant-giving organizations), many of the tasks are the same for nonprofits (generally grant-seeking organizations), and the list is valuable for its view of the work and positions one may find in the nonprofit sector. When reviewing the list, note that many of the management and tracking functions would be the same in many nonprofits; for some, it would be of outgoing grants, for others, of incoming donations. See also chapter 4, "Meeting People Who Made It: Some Case Histories," for a bit more insight to the nature of the work and positions in the sector.

Experience, Diversity, and Job Crossover

There is a particular richness and colorfulness to this sector's diversity. The work ranges from the arts to the environment, from education to health care. It can be people intensive or allow for reflection, study, and research. There is more room in this sector for diverse skills and interests than any other.

If among your work "tools" exists a strong awareness of political, social, ethnic, and racial communities, you may be particularly well suited for the nonprofit sector. Having a healthy respect for the educational, cultural, and economic diversity of our society is one good leg up on working well in this sector.

On the other hand, there appears to be a growing propensity among those hiring in the sector to look for increasing levels of academic achievement both for entry positions or as one requirement for moving up the job ladder. For the most part these requirements are master's degrees in a given discipline such as social work or public health. However, before you despair because you don't have a master's in whatever, take heart that there appears to remain considerable room for persons whose life experience substitutes for formal academic training or who can acquire such training on the job.

Many of you will be pleased to know that there is considerable job crossover in this sector, an opportunity to perform your same job in a nonprofit setting. It is quite possible to work in the nonprofit sector while continuing to practice your current craft as a secretary, accountant, attorney, or administrator, to name just a few.

Every job in the sector is not unique. Many of them are very similar to private sector or government jobs—but they are executed in a different context.

Figure 3-2: Sample list of job titles and definitions

Chief Executive Officer: Responsible for directing the overall program and administrative activities of the foundation. Responsible for the effective use of financial and human resources of the foundation.

Associate Director or Vice President (General): Number two person. Responsible for directing more than one major program or administrative activity of the foundation. Exercises discretionary power in significant matters, and is designated the officer in charge of the foundation's daily activities in the absence of the CEO.

Vice President (Program): Responsible for directing the program activities of the foundation, including the grantmaking program, special projects, or programs operated by the foundation. Responsible for establishing policies and procedures to manage programs.

Vice President (Administration): Responsible for directing the internal administrative activities of the foundation, personnel, and office administration. May also oversee financial activities in some organizations. Responsible for establishing policies and procedures to manage support activities.

Secretary of the Corporation: Responsible for corporate records. May also be responsible for handling legal matters if there is not a general counsel.

Treasurer (Chief Financial Officer): Responsible for directing the financial/accounting activities, including investment management or monitoring outside investment management.

Secretary/Treasurer: Responsible for the duties of both positions as outlined above.

Controller: Responsible for operation of financial and bookkeeping services, including preparation of financial analyses, income and expense reports, budgets, and governmental reports. May also be responsible for directing purchasing, payroll, other financial operations.

Investment Officer: Manages investment assets. May oversee outside investment managers.

General Counsel: Responsible for directing the legal activities of the foundation. Responsible for coordinating legal matters with outside counsel, and for advising staff on legal matters pertaining to the foundation.

Assistant Vice President/Assistant Director: Provides professional-level assistance to vice president or associate director for duties out-

Figure 3-2: Sample list of job titles and definitions (con't)

lined under Associate Director or Vice President (Administration) above.

Assistant Secretary: Provides professional assistance to corporate secretary for duties outlined under Secretary of the Corporation above.

Assistant Treasurer: Provides professional assistance to treasurer for duties outlined under Treasurer (Chief Financial Officer) above.

Assistant Controller: Provides professional assistance to controller for duties outlined under Controller above.

Program Director: Responsible for managing the grantmaking program of a particular subject area (education, arts/humanities, health, etc.) or geographic region. In larger-staffed foundations, a senior-level program officer who supervises other program staff in carrying out grantmaking or in-house programs. Recommends (or has authority to approve in some cases) distribution of grant dollars within budget for the program area.

Program Officer: Responsible for investigating and evaluating grant proposals and/or carrying out in-house projects. In larger-staffed foundations this may involve one subject area or geographic region. In smaller foundation program officers are usually responsible for most aspects of the grantmaking process (including program research, proposal evaluation, grant tracking, post-grant evaluation, etc.).

Program Associate: Evaluates grant proposals, does background research and prepares for funding. Is often an entry-level program officer position in larger-staffed foundations.

Communications Officer: Responsible for directing the communications activities of the foundation, including publications, public/press relations, production of annual report. Establishes policies and practices to develop and maintain the desired image of the foundation.

Fund Raising Officer: In community foundations only—responsible for establishing and maintaining fund raising efforts to the foundation. May have responsibility for other donee relations activities.

Research Professional: Responsible for directing the foundation's research activities or for carrying out foundation-funded research projects. Often part of a fellowship or in-house operating research program.

Figure 3-2: Sample list of job titles and definitions (con't)

Computer Professional: Responsible for programming, data processing, or database management activities. May assist other staff (financial, grants managers, others) in using the foundation's computer equipment.

Office Manager: Responsible for operation and maintenance of all facilities. Develops, recommends, and implements policies and procedures for office operation and often for personnel policies.

Librarian: Manages in-house library and may assist program staff by doing background research.

Accountant: Maintains financial record systems; provides auditing services and financial statements to the foundation managers.

Program Assistant: Assists the program officers with proposal evaluation and provides some administrative support. May also keep track of grants if there is no grants manager.

Research Assistant: Assists research professional with duties outlined in Research Professional above, and provides some administrative support.

Financial Assistant/Bookkeeper: Provides a variety of recordkeeping services to accountant, controller, or others managing the foundation's finances.

Grants Manager: Keeps track of grants made by the foundation, obtaining and managing reports required from grantees.

Administrative Assistant: Performs a variety of responsible clerical duties requiring independent analysis, judgment and knowledge of foundation or departmental functions. Maintains records, processes complex documents, compiles regular and special reports.

Secretary: Performs standard secretarial functions. Includes executive, administrative, other secretarial positions.

Word Processing Operator: Produces typed copy on automated office equipment.

Clerk: Includes file, mail clerks, clerk-typists, and other clerical positions.

Receptionist: Greets visitors, handles switchboard. May also do typing and related clerical tasks.

Reprinted with permission from *1985 Foundation Compensation Report*, The Council on Foundations, June 1985, Washington, D.C. This report contains tables of information of high, low, mean, and median salary by position title at asset levels and for geographic regions, especially useful if you are leaning towards a foundation job.

THE SPECIAL CHARACTERISTICS OF WORK IN THE SECTOR

The Imperative of Commitment

For many of us in the sector, caring about what we are doing in a significant way is more important than the image of the institution, its location, and even the nature of the work itself. Underlying people's performance of jobs in the sector are several driving forces that propelled them to the nonprofit workplace in the first place, forces that can be summarized as "commitment."

At the core of the most nonprofit workers' rationale for having chosen to work in this sector is a deep-rooted concern for people. And it goes beyond just "people." As Arthur Himmelman, the Associate Director of the McKnight Foundation of St. Paul, Minnesota, recently said, "one of the three key things most valued about working in the nonprofit sector is the ability "'to be recognized for my ability to use highly professional skills on behalf of those who would not normally have access to them.'"

A second common drive running through many people's feelings in the nonprofit sector about their job functions is the desire, indeed demand, for a fairly high ethical content to their work. As the same Arthur Himmelman put it, there is a strong need "to feel that ethical issues are of major importance and that the primary activity of the organization is to assist those in need."

A third common drive, though more difficult to measure even in the anecdotal method in which I have gathered some of the material for this section, is the sense that many of the people who labor in this sector value a sense of "feeling good" about what they do. Ms. Joan Welsh, the Director of the Boulder County Safe House, a shelter for battered women, and the Chair of the National Coalition Against Domestic Violence, a coalition of shelters for battered women and children, quoted a wonderful Sufi saying when we talked about her work: "Let what you do be what you love. There are hundreds of ways to kneel and kiss the earth."

Also important to many nonprofit sector workers is to find in their place of work a group of compatible and caring colleagues. These people value working with others who share their vision of how the world should operate—and, perhaps of greater import, how the world should *be*. As Mr. Tom Layton, Executive Director of the Gerbod Foundation in San Francisco recently said to me: "I like the idealism, the sense of working on large and important issues, and, most of all, companionship and relationship with others in the sector. Without wanting to push the generalization too far, I find nonprofit types more interesting . . . ."

Another key qualitative factor common in most NPOs is an emphasis on service. Many nonprofit workers think about their occupations as providing them with an opportunity to serve others. A growing number of us even view leadership in service terms. One of my first "required readings," for a new person on our foundation's program staff is *The Servant as a Leader*, by Robert Greenleaf. Mr. Greenleaf has many useful things to say about leadership and they seem particularly applicable to the nonprofit sector. For example, he says, "A new moral principle is emerging which holds that the only authority deserving one's allegiance is that which is freely and knowingly granted by the led to the leader in response to, and in proportion to, the clearly evident servant stature of the leader. Those who choose to follow this principle will not casually accept the authority of existing institutions. *Rather, they will freely respond only to individuals who are chosen as leaders because they are proven and trusted as servants.*"[2]

A slightly different observation on our work in this sector is that it seems to permit and at times command a bit more of one's self. Said another way, you don't just "do" many of the nonprofit sector jobs. In at least some serious way, many people in the sector *live* some aspect of their work.

From the perspective of the potential new worker in the sector, there are a variety of options in carrying out many of the tasks of importance to NPOs in the sector. Many of the tasks can be implemented at a highly sophisticated level by professionals, managed by administrative or managerial personnel, carried out by paraprofessionals, or in a number of instances, engaged in at some level by volunteers. Thus, the prospective employee is presented with a rich and diverse matrix of employment possibilities, each requiring different levels of commitment and involvement in the work process.

The Demands of Size and Complexity

As we have discussed elsewhere in this book, there is a considerable spread in the size and complexity of nonprofit organizations within the sector. The implications of this for the work are that a potential worker's functions can range from managing extremely large and complex organizations or working in them to, for example, being the sole employee of a storefront information and referral organization that addresses the drug use problems of young people.

Thus, the functions you are likely to perform as an employee can range from being extremely well (and narrowly) defined in larger and more bureaucratic organizations, to being the "chief cook and bottle washer" in the small organization.

The choice, from your point of view, may depend upon how much flexibility and variety you wish to have in your work. The smaller, more flexible organizations also tend to be less well capitalized and as a result generally can afford to spend less on the compensation and skill development of their personnel. Yet these smaller organizations are often the locus of exciting, stimulating work and considerable responsibility early on, even for the new employee.

Although there is a considerable range in NPO size and complexity, the average NPO is much smaller than its government or private sector counterpart. As a result, very few NPOs can offer either sufficient scale of operations or growth potential to provide prospective employees with career ladders without at least a few of the rungs missing. This may be an advantage to our sector!

Stress in the Sector

Similar to the issue of complexity are the levels of stress in some organizations in the nonprofit sector. The work is by no means all cheerful, easy-going, "doing good" from nine to five. Some of the stress comes from attempting to address major social problems without enough resources. Other stress sources come directly from the nature of the work. For example, the executive directors and workers in the shelters for battered women and children, have jobs extremely high in stress content. One of their few compensations (they don't get paid much in cash) is the extraordinary high psychic reward of helping their fellow human beings reach safety and shelter at times of extreme stress, family difficulty, or extreme physical and psychological fear and danger. The nurses and orderlies in the Saturday night emergency rooms of hospitals also experience heavy stress. So do the social workers in drug rehabilitation programs and the nurse's aides in frail and elderly visitation efforts.

As is true for most workers in other fields, there is a range of human capacity to cope with stress. The key for you as a prospective new employee will be to make judgments about this important factor and the many wonderful tradeoffs that come with it. As Ms. Lois Roisman, Executive Director of the Jewish Fund for Justice, Washington, D.C., puts it, "It is hard to find a good time to leave a good job, but there is an intense burnout factor at work in this business and you have to stay fresh. Stay with something long enough to make a difference."

Upward Mobility

While it is extremely difficult to generalize with any validity about upward mobility in the sector, and since upward movement takes place at the individual organizational level, many of the NPOs in some nonprofit sector segments are fairly limited in the upward mobility they provide due to their limited growth and low staff turnover. This situation, especially for younger people at the beginning of their careers, calls for greater mobility between segments of the nonprofit sector as well as an openness to intersector transfers from time to time.

The other implication of this situation for the younger person is to raise the premium on education and training that expands the individual's general capacities and leads to greater job flexibility.

Again, it is risky to generalize about the sector, or even its major segments. You should explore the issue of upward mobility with each nonprofit organization for which you consider working. In addition, you should also attempt to develop some judgment (without exploring the subject in a great deal of detail) about what kind of transferable skills and experience you will acquire in prospective positions. One approach to exploring this sensitive topic is to ask what has happened over the years to the people who have performed well in this organization. Have they moved up into management? Have they transferred to other, larger organizations? Have they left this segment of the sector or the sector itself altogether? It is appropriate to explore those questions since your frame of reference is one of hoping to find a career more than a job and determining what the prospects for promotion and increased responsibility are within the organization you are considering.

Key Challenges

The sector faces a number of key challenges and difficulties.[3] While we can identify some of them, it is also important to recognize that there are very large gaps in data regarding work in the sector and who carries it out. Nonetheless, a few of the more useful ones for you to explore, whether you are new to the sector or simply contemplating a job change within the sector are:

1. *Many organizations lack real and adequately planned or financed training opportunities.* "Typically, we are tossed into these tremendous responsibilities without sufficient training or on-the-job supervision."[4]

2. *Many of the sector's managers, although good at their jobs and highly dedicated, arrive at their positions without as much formal training as they might like.* As one small foundation executive director recently said in response to a question about what she might have done differently, "I would have had a stronger academic preparation . . . .I find that the issues I'm dealing with would be better served by me if I had a stronger background in economics."

3. *One must relate to a comparatively large number of people ranging from agency staff, clients, board members, funders (government and private), and people in the community.* Note, however, that this variety and change is also the spice and stimulation of the sector.

4. *Attempts to reconcile limited resources with seemingly unlimited human needs are often frustrating.* But, this challenge also has its flipside in the joy of helping others, albeit with limited resources.

5. *Staffs and boards both tend to exaggerate what their organizations can do.* Wishing doesn't make it so. There is considerable burnout and stress in the sector from people who would like to help more but do not have the resources to do so.

6. *The environment is much less structured,* resulting in higher levels of frustration for those who prefer a life on the more orderly side of the spectrum.

7. *There is not adequate upward mobility or room for sufficient horizontal transfers in some sector subsegments.* Of course, the private and government sectors share this problem as well.

8. *The financial rewards don't always match the responsibilities* the way they tend to in the private and public sectors because most NPOs are small and underfinanced.

9. *Because a number of NPOs are working in critical human service areas, the jobs may well not end at 5, 6, or even 8 p.m.* The hours can be long in service-delivery organizations. And, meetings with volunteer boards of directors or volunteer supplements to staff may take place after the volunteers *"normal"* working hours.

Unique Qualities and Opportunities

Finally there are some special, unique qualities of the work here in the nonprofit sector. They may add some additional texture to your perspective on the sector. On the plus side, for example:

- Status is not defined by one's credentials in this sector as much as in others.
- There is more room and opportunity for generalists.
- More of the work is project-oriented, enabling the nonprofit worker to see more of the final results of his/her work and providing more of a feeling of "wholeness" about one's work.
- The scale of organizations is usually smaller, increasing the intimacy of many working relationships.
- Conceptual work plays a stronger role enabling more attention to be paid to ideas and issues.

On the minus side, however:

- Undercapitalization is more widespread, making it more difficult to borrow to test new ideas.
- There is less vigorous investment in human capital and equipment.
- There is greater reliance on soft (and sometimes illusory) sources of operating funds thus reducing job security.

Now let's turn to compensation, benefits, and security.

THE REWARDS: COMPENSATION, BENEFITS, AND SECURITY

Although I am an acknowledged fan of the nonprofit sector, it is important for me to ensure that you do not embark on a career search without knowing that "it isn't all a bed of roses out here." To put it more bluntly, there are a number of less attractive factors about this sector's reward structure (though they are generalizations) that readers should recognize as they begin their job search. These include the facts that:

- Pay is generally lower than in the private sector though the gap is slowly closing. Yet there are growing numbers of people happily working on issues they care about deeply *and* earning a very respectable living. For example, a major metropolitan United Way's 1985 salary survey noted maximum annual salary rates ranging from junior clerks at $12,864 to senior executives at $90,264; a 1985 survey of foundations by the Council of Foundations[5] found annual salaries in the nonprofits ranging from $10,000 to $22,500 for clerks and from $12,000 to $210,000 for chief executive officers, depending on whether the foundation was independent, corporate, private, community, or public.

- Fringe benefits as a whole package are either nonexistent or much less when compared with private and public sector organizations. The benefit packages in nonprofit organizations are an extremely mixed bag. When compared with the other sectors, a number of NPOs offer a better deal in the areas of vacations (relatively longer), working hours (more flexible), and work apparel (less formal, i.e., less expensive). On the other hand, many NPOs do not measure up to the offerings of the other sectors when it comes to life insurance, pension/retirement programs, or adequate medical/dental coverage.
- The physical surroundings of many NPOs are not as attractive or conducive to one's best work. The work places are often more crowded, older, less well equipped, *but* they are often closer to the action and can be far more exciting places to work.
- Less attention and fewer resources are devoted to the development of the human capital of the sector. More specifically, comparatively less attention is paid to recruitment, training, career development, further inservice training, graduate education, and so on.
- Mobility, either upward, or even at times, horizontal, can be somewhat limited because of relatively slower organizational growth rates and lower turnover of existing personnel.
- Because of limited oversight by boards of directors, some senior executives in the nonprofit sector can be a bit shortsighted by refusing to build and train younger people below them. A minority of these executives and midlevel administrators, without board intervention or encouragement, can refuse to delegate any meaningful level or amount of authority. Mr. Pablo Eisenberg, the Executive Director of the Washington, D.C.-based Center for Community Change once put it fairly bluntly: Some nonprofit organizations can experience "worse problems with succession than Louis XIV."

On the other hand, the people cited in this book and my professional colleagues are overwhelmingly pleased with their work and are eager for new challenges!

NOTES
Chapter 3

1. Richard N. Bolles, *What Color is Your Parachute? A Practical Manual for Job Hunters and Career Changers* (Berkeley, Calif.: Ten Speed Press, 1984), 77.

2. Robert K. Greenleaf, *Servant Leadership: A Journey Into the Nature of Legitimate Power and Greatness*, (New York: New York's Paulist Press, 1977), 10.

3. For a more complete discussion of several of these issues, see Brian O'Connell, "It Takes a 'Different Animal' to Succeed in Nonprofit Management," *The Nonprofit Executive* (Washington, D.C.: The Taft Group, June 1983), 3-4.

4. Ibid.

5. James A. Joseph, Elizabeth T. Boris, and Carol A. Hooper, *1985 Foundation Compensation Report*, (Washington, D.C.: The Council on Foundations, Inc., 1985).

CHAPTER 4

MEETING PEOPLE WHO MADE IT: SOME CASE HISTORIES

Getting to know individuals who work in the sector is a good way to learn about how and why others got started on a nonprofit career. This series of informal interviews was conducted with people holding positions at various job levels in nonprofit organizations throughout the sector. The people surveyed here are indexed by name, job title, and geographic location in appendix D.

Project Manager and Consultant

Jerry Cronin is Project Manager at Independent Community Consultants, Inc., a nonprofit management support/technical assistance organization based in Hampton, Arkansas.

"I decided exactly how to set upon a career in the NPO sector during a college orientation for VISTA volunteers. I saw a need for a vehicle to orchestrate social change efforts in East Tennessee and, with a half-dozen close friends, formed Big Oranges for a Democratic Society ('BODS') in Knoxville, planned and managed its growth and, after one year, offered our newly discovered expertise to the McCarthy campaign, Black Student Union, Poor People's Campaign, etc. When pausing to reflect on this, I realize that the 'BODS' experience actually became, three years later, Independent Community Consultants, Inc. (ICC). Without groping in the dark with 'BODS,' I'd not have had the confidence later to set up ICC. I learned that the nonprofit community is most accepting of vital diverse ideas—and folks willing to 'give it a try.'" His work evolved into consulting and problem solving for grass roots groups around the country.

"I value the ability of the sector to cause positive, dramatic social change locally and globally, the ability of many folks in the sector to think of their 'job' as a 'career' characterized by service to others rather than service to self, the independence and ability of groups to respond to changing environments quickly, and the sense of ethics that often pervades the sector."

Jerry worked as a volunteer in high school with the Mothers' March for Birth Defects, the Heart Fund, and Voter Registration Drives, and later, in fund raising for social change efforts. To a question on what preparation he might recommend for work in the sector, he responds that one should get a good grounding in liberal arts *and* business, and that it is important to participate in apprenticeships and internships "while in college that feature work (licking envelopes, knocking on doors, changing sheets) that gives one a sense of starting at the bottom in order to remember it later at the top, where the perspective may be applied."

"Recognize that there are lots of jobs for you in the sector *if* you are willing to:

- move
- study
- accept challenges
- generalize your particular experience to other jobs and disciplines.

"Change jobs before you have to change—be smart and monitor your own motivation, stress and dedication.

"Find the job you want and go after it with a vengeance. Forsake financial reward in return for a terrific job that lets you use all your skills. Have an aggressive program of interdisciplinary continuing education that you pursue so that you offer employers a more complete person."

Fund-Raising Consultant

Phyllis Quan, of D'Agostino, Underwood, Quan, and Associates, a fund-raising consulting firm in San Diego, California, had always done volunteer work while going to school, did summer research throughout graduate school, and had just finished her qualifying exam for her Ph.D. when she applied for and was offered a three-month summer consultant job with the California Council for the Humanities (CCH) in program development with minority communities. Her work with community-based nonprofits and universities led to a full-time position with CCH as a program officer in San Francisco. She attributes this success to a combination of her volunteer and academic interests, and the job that followed (as Executive Director of ARCO Foundation) to networking done during her three years with CCH. Please note that she was also very good at her work *and* worked very hard.

"Use every opportunity you can to help your organization and expand your own skills at the same time. Networking can help your organization and your future. Do a good job in your current job, and focus on how to market the organization's services and programs, rather than on inward issues.

"I have learned of the broad range of careers in the nonprofit sector. The work is demanding, challenging, and rewarding. Those thinking of careers in the sector should do volunteer work, learn how to be an effective volunteer. Test your commitment to it."

Her advice to those seeking nonprofit sector work stresses:

- *Preparation.* Talk to people currently working in the nonprofit sector and read up on the sector (through the publications of the Foundation Center, Nonprofit Management Association, VOLUNTEER, etc.). While in school develop good written and verbal communication skills. Take some management and communication courses. Do volunteer work. Develop a resume focusing on your most transferable skills.
- *Contacts.* Define your current network of contacts, selectively choose those who represent diverse spheres of influence, talk to them and give them a sense of the kind of work environment in which you are interested.
- *Interviews.* Practice. You might not be 100 percent interested in every job, but every interview gives you good practice. You may be surprised by what you learn. Know as much as you can about the organization before the interview. Pose questions as well as answering them.
- *Identification.* Look for a good match for yourself in terms of management, style, growth potential, and potential for creativity. Learn from others about the organization.
- *Talking.* Talk to as many people as you can.

"[There is] potential in the sector for creativity and for use of my communication/catalytic skills. I can effect change, help organizations build their capacity and be instrumental in getting others to think in new ways."

Vice President, Community Foundation

James R. Dumpson is Vice President, New Community Trust, the community foundation for New York City. He has administered the human services systems of New York City twice and was formerly

Dean of the Graduate School of Social Work at Fordham University, former chair of the National Association of Social Workers and holder of many, many other line, staff, and honorary positions.

"I would recommend a basic liberal arts education and education for a particular job function or set of functions. I would recommend that one keep in mind the likelihood of changing jobs/careers three or four times during one's working life. That requires education, and testing for new areas to pursue—taking courses, maybe first to satisfy the needs of a hobby, finding interest and satisfaction and then serious pursuit of a new field while maybe maintaining or improving skill in one's field. Career planning, consciously done, is essential for meaningful career building. Of course, values underlie all of this. To what values is one committed? These values influence one's choices in career building. The values, I suggest, should be explicit to the individual.

"I was drawn to return to a local neighborhood center whenever I could for the encouragement and insight into needs of under-privileged youth that it had given me. My motivation was twofold: to pay society back and help other youths, and to earn money to return to college. I became a youth worker in the 8th Ward Settlement House, an enclave of hard-working, poor, and neglected black families, in Philadelphia, Pennsylvania, organized by the Society of Friends, whose philosophy influenced my role in the nonprofit sector in later life.

"As I reflect, [it was necessary to] be intuitively in the right place at the right time, inquisitive about different work settings without any idea of working in any one of them, like to meet people and build relationships, relate to their interests, and maintain a level, however low, of visibility on whatever job I was in.

"The 'generalist' that *was* the model employee in the not-for-profit sector is no longer (as widely) accepted: (a) specialization within the sector is a must; (b) mobility now characterizes the sector; the sector requires freedom to relocate if one is to take advantage of job opportunities; (c) competition is keener as more and more skilled specialists become available; and (d) ongoing training and skill development are now essential—familiarity with the contributions of technology, new ways of using oneself in one's job is a challenge to one's ability to change, even when one is 'on top.'

"[There is] a minimum of bureaucratic 'overload' [in the work in the sector], association with growing, creative people and a minimum of 'burnout' evident, and individualization, reflected in recognition (not necessarily monetary) of a job well done."

Executive Director, Fund

Lois Roisman is now Executive Director of the Jewish Fund for Justice in Washington, D.C. Her career began with learning about all segments of Oklahoma City life and translating that knowledge into community foundation work as a volunteer. This volunteer work served as the basis for her resume for her first job, as an assistant to a friend who was the Executive Director of the Oklahoma City Community Foundation.

She believes that had she had a chance to do it differently, she would have had stronger academic preparation. Specifically, economics would have helped her to address better the issues with which she currently deals. And she emphasizes the need for some level of specialization. Lois has spent considerable time with young people who have come to Washington, D.C. right out of college, but who have nothing to give them any advantage over others. "Graduate school in a field of expertise such as geriatrics, economics, or social policy would help."

Lois Roisman also sees a randomness of funding patterns in the sector that comes from policies that aren't thoroughly conceived. "There is a trendiness in the foundation (and nonprofit) world that is seductive but must be resisted, otherwise we're left with issues begun to be addressed but left to wander the streets just like the mental patients we had 'deinstitutionalized,' but tired of in a few years."

She values her work as a rare opportunity to merge personal philosophy and public work. She values the freedom, and "the opportunity to make a real difference in the lives of others."

Lois suggests that one may view work with smaller organizations as creating possibilities, that she has heard others in the sector advise young aspirants to go to New York where the foundations are, but that her experience reminds her that "you can start as a big fish in a little pond first and then advance in foundation (and other nonprofit) life, because it's a small community, and everyone knows what others are doing in all areas of the country." This is particularly true in the smaller subsegments of the sector, but then the *whole* sector is smaller and more intimate, in the main.

Executive Director, Foundation

Tom Layton is Executive Director, The Wallace Alexander Gerbode Foundation in San Francisco.

In 1971, the Coro Foundation in San Francisco, a program to train people interested in public affairs, was financially failing and looking at closing a number of its projects. Tom Layton viewed the offer to serve as Vice President in charge of administration and fund raising on a national basis as exciting and an opportunity to be useful in helping a troubled organization.

"I like the idealism, the sense of working on large and important issues, and, most of all, companionship and relationships with others in the sector. I measure a lot of my life in terms of how I spend my time and who I spend it with.

"It is my impression that, over the past fifteen years, the non-profit sector has developed some sort of definition. The degree of professionalism has increased tremendously. The larger organizations are well managed, and managed by individuals who often are highly qualified and well paid. On the other end of the scale, many small organizations still are not in the position to offer decent compensation and are often staffed with people who learn on the job and who have little or no experience."

Tom responds to the question on what preparation he would recommend for work in the nonprofit sector as tied to one specific field of interest. "Many areas of nonprofit work are highly professionalized. More generally, the nonprofit sector relies even more heavily on relationships, contacts, personality traits, etc. than does the for-profit sector. Political skills are important. Anyone who is considering changing jobs should do all he/she can to develop relationships, competencies, and expertise beyond one's individual agency.

Regarding opportunities for women, Tom points out that "It seems that there are a large number of highly talented women in nonprofit work. I've seen many women gain important experience and quickly shoulder significant responsibilities in nonprofit work." Tom also illustrates by word and his own professional life the enormous leverage that can be acquired through building and maintaining a large network of persons who know, trust, and rely on your work.

Executive Director, Shelter

Joan Welsh is Executive Director of the Boulder County Safe House, Boulder, Colorado, a shelter for battered women and the Chair of the National Coalition Against Domestic Violence, a coalition of shelters for battered women and children.

"Gaining work experience as a volunteer is extremely valid and important. More and more organizations are managing volunteers as professionals, which benefits both the organization and individual volunteer." She began thinking about nonprofit sector work "when my children were well into school age." And her part-time volunteer work at Boulder County Women's Resource Center in Colorado became full time and paying eight months later. "I had the luxury of working as a volunteer in a nonprofit agency whose goals, politics, and idealogy I supported. I then worked into a paying position when it opened. I have seen this repeated frequently where volunteers who prove to be creative and responsible workers are in a prime position when a paid position opens. It also gives a person a chance to try out an organization before committing to it full time. This has also been my experience in my current position.

"I also took every workshop available to me to upgrade my skills, i.e., Grantwriting, Crisis Intervention, and Managing Volunteers. I searched for courses through local universities and technical assistance centers. Of further help was talking with everyone I could think of who could teach me what I didn't know. I was never shy about asking questions and going to others I admired to find out how they did it."

She coordinated the establishment of a shelter for battered women, which included obtaining a house and city and county zoning approvals, grant writing, fund raising, public relations, volunteer recruitment and supervision, hiring staff, and program design and development.

"I have found that skills transfer easily from one nonprofit organization to another. Issues change, but management is basically the same.

"Learn all you can regarding the specific issue or organization in which you are interested. Read literature on the issue, research the organization in the library, talk to people knowledgeable in its background history. Visit the organization; volunteer there; talk with current and past employees. Be clear as to the mission of the organization and the prospective job description.

"Think creatively and in depth regarding how you see the job. Visualize yourself doing the job and what that would mean to you and to the organization.

"When interviewing, show yourself to be the person you are. Try to express your values as well as concrete work ideas; humor is always valuable, too.

"Talk to people in a community to find out how organizations are perceived (i.e., United Way, other organizations that interface, service recipients). Research the community; keep in touch with people in the nonprofit work force."

And what she values most about her work in the sector is working with people who share her vision of the world, making social and personal change, and "working to change the world for the better."

Associate Director, Foundation

Arthur Himmelman is Associate Director of the McKnight Foundation in St. Paul, Minnesota. He began work in the sector as a Research Fellow at the Center for Urban and Regional Affairs, University of Minnesota, in 1968. Arthur was doing action research, designing, organizing, and coordinating storefront university programs in inner-city neighborhoods. "I knew professors who were working on urban poverty issues, and I had been very active in raising equity issues regarding education for the disadvantaged as a student 'movement' leader. I showed a great deal of interest in, and was a strong advocate for, special community-based programs. I was anxious and highly motivated to work in inner-city communities.

For the career changer and job hunter Arthur recommends that you: "Think seriously about convincing someone to hire you to do what you really think needs to be done; that is, do not simply look for jobs listed, but talk with people about your own ideas and see if they might not be able to create opportunities, even if part time initially; that might allow you to focus on both your skills and interests. Sometimes taking a job in this sector that is too far from your ethical or professional comfort level will discourage you from any further commitments in the sector.

"I would underscore the need to have a strong point of view or approach to problem solving that has both philosophical and practical clarity: the 'why' and 'how' issues. Balance the philosophical and the practical. Because most people are very much on one side of this equation or the other, you will be noticed for your integration of these crucial factors.

"The work is complex in its specializations, and in its need for multifaceted approaches to client and organizational problems. The range of resources that have emerged also requires that a person be more broadly familiar with approaches to problem solving than may be a part of his/her own formal training.

"I would suggest service on nonprofit organizational boards as a good background for a career orientation in the nonprofit sector. This can provide a good overview of the range of problems and issues that you could face in your own area of practice.

"I would also strongly suggest that one think very carefully about his/her own world view or basic assumptions before becoming committed to this kind of work. It is too easy to lose sight of the fundamental reasons for activity in this sector given the daily weight of problems one must address."

Arthur believes that ethical issues are of major importance and that the primary role of the nonprofit organization should be to assist those in need. He sees the advantages of working in the sector as the opportunity to be recognized for his ability to use highly professional skills on behalf of those to whom these are normally inaccessible, and to be stimulated by opportunities for new learning. Arthur has also experienced a number of opportunities to improve the practice of his profession. He advises against selling yourself too strongly and the values for which you stand too little. Your accomplishments should be discussed in terms of the people who have been assisted, rather than in terms of what "I" did.

Director, Sexual Abuse Center

Kee MacFarlane, Director, Child Sexual Abuse Diagnostic Center, Children's Institute International (CII), Los Angeles, California, extends similar vision, sentiments, and advice toward work in the nonprofit sector as those before. She adds that there is a time to move on. If your skills at something are the best they can be and there are no new opportunities, consider documenting it, passing it on to others, and developing something new. Job changes just for the new perspectives and skills can broaden you and make what you do more valuable. It might have to do with keeping some vision of what still needs to be done and what you can do in the right circumstances. Opportunities are usually created.

She followed her natural and initial instincts in obtaining her first job in the sector, and looked in the classified ads for work with children. The job for which she interviewed, and got, directed her "and completely changed the course of my career.

"It frequently stretches me to produce to the maximum of my abilities. I've learned I can do a lot more things than I ever thought I could." Kee was modest in her interview. From her work at California's CII, she and her colleagues have had an enormous impact on how communities deal with the social, emotional, and legal traumas of large scale sexual abuse cases, especially those involving younger children. Kee, and other women and men like her, are helping our society face one of its darker sides more constructively.

Planning Director, United Way

Terri Barreiro is the Director of Planning, Allocations and Evaluation, the United Way of the Minneapolis Area, Minneapolis, Minnesota. She was at first primarily concerned with working with people, regardless of whether the sector was nonprofit or for-profit. She admires the breadth of the people involved in nonprofit work, believing that the sector contains "more 'color,' a broader age range, and more acceptance of people as they are." However, she also sees aspects of the sector as inefficient and with an unwillingness to act— "too much talk," and as undercapitalized.

She had been a student volunteer with a nonprofit organization and was subsequently offered full-time and paying work. She advises volunteering in the sector while working in order to serve the organization or cause, to strengthen social interaction, and to build the professional network. In addition, she emphasizes a willingness to change jobs regularly (perhaps after four to five years) and building one's people and public decision-making skills. She also emphasizes strong writing, communication, and problem-analysis skills.

Office Manager, Nonprofit Training Organization

Saralei Farner is currently the Office Manager of the Southern California Center for Nonprofit Management in my home town of Los Angeles, California. The Center is a very important technical assistance and training outfit ably directed by Alan Kumamoto and his talented associate Patti Oertle.

Saralei is a vital member of the Center's administrative team. She works in the nerve center of an organization which must tactfully, discerningly and quickly deal with a daily onslaught of calls and letters from clients who are both individuals and organizations plus inquiries from government officials, current and potential funders, the Center's Board of Directors and many others. They run numerous training programs, a management consulting operation plus several very promising service projects such as the Southern California Energy Conservation Program—a collaborative project in cooperation with a progressive local utility that helps nonprofit organizations identify, finance and implement energy conservation measures that will save them significant money over the long haul.

Saralei, through her considerable experience in nine different positions in three countries, all in the nonprofit sector, suggests that there are a variety of promising avenues to stimulating jobs in this sector, including by:

- "Moving geographically and working up from local units through regional offices to national headquarters." Please note that not all national headquarters are in Washington D.C. or New York City, especially as the philanthropic action shifts West and South.
- "Securing referrals from colleagues and associates over the years; building and maintaining a network of (high quality) contacts is very important.
- Believing in an organization's mission and wanting to work for it and selling yourself into a job.

Saralei is good at her many crafts. I suspect one of the reasons is that she likes her work and her colleagues. Saralei comments that "work at the local level is a lot more fun and provides a very personal sense of community belonging and participation." She points out that it is "easier to see results of your work at the local level where you deal with actual constituents . . ."

Saralei represents thousands of dedicated, skilled workers in this sector in her love of its values and that special learning that can take place when one turns one's attention to the needs of others. Recently she wrote to me saying "The nonprofit organizations I have worked for over the last 35 years have required that I learn new skills, new ways of work, and working with new groups of people, often under less than desirable conditions. A job that is static wouldn't be any fun for me. I also had the opportunity of traveling and working all over the USA and in other countries . . ." And she has really been there, ". . . from flood relief on Christmas Day to taking constituents to tea at the White House. Some of it has been done in other languages in foreign cultures. And almost all of it was worth getting up for in the morning." Saralei always trys to be a missionary for our cause, but is savvy enough to know that "it's a long crusade."

Saralei had lots of useful advice for job seekers. I have selected a sample of her suggestions:

- "Get the best education you can afford—preferably liberal arts with any specialty you like . . . In the nonprofit world you have to be able to converse with every segment of society, and a good education and some experience of 'life' in high school and college years are very helpful.

53

- Continue your education. Attend workshops, get an advanced degree, read the daily newspaper and professional journals.
- Be willing to use your strong back as well as your mind. Move chairs, serve coffee, do whatever has to be done. Be willing to learn something new and to attempt things that may be beyond your reach when required. You'll learn how to do it in the process.
- Look for a good mentor whom you admire and respect and learn from him/her. A good boss who is willing to let you learn is worth your annual raise in the long run.
- Be very honest about your marketable skills and *for whom* and *where* you are willing to use them. Start out with a cause/ organization that you really want to work for—believing in the mission is absolutely essential to success.
- Be absolutely honest and careful about managing all funds raised by your organization regardless of the source."

Like so many of her talented nonprofit colleagues, Saralei is a "perfectly charming person, well read, has a box at the Bowl, supports her alma mater, and is going to Cambridge University this summer." She practices what she preaches. And she values Quakers. So do I.

Adjunct Professor, Graduate School of Public Affairs, and Executive Director, Family Foundation

Robert Leduc is an Adjunct Professor at the Graduate School of Public Affairs, University of Colorado at Denver, and the Executive Director of the Anshutz Family Foundations. Bob actually wears a third hat as the President of the nonprofit Institute for Nonprofit Organization Management.

He developed his interest in the sector during graduate school after a tour in the military. His initial interest was in providing volunteer technical support to community-based nonprofit organizations. He landed his first job in the sector by inventing it! He served initially as a volunteer Executive Director of the Accounting Aid Society of Metropolitan Detroit. The job had not existed before. Then, when the position was funded, he was there!

Like many of his colleagues, Bob values in particular the fact that:

- "The net effect of my career makes America/Denver a better place to live. We're changing things for the better."
- He likes "the policy orientation of this field. As a whole, we are trying to do things that are worth doing for Americans."

Bob's advice to job seekers covers a number of important topics. He particularly suggests that job seekers:

- "Secure educational experience specific to nonprofit organizations at the graduate level.
- Arrange an internship between your graduate school and a local branch of a large/important NPO.
- Network—get to know people in NPOs. Get them to introduce you to others in the field.
- Develop strong job-seeking tools (e.g., resume, bio sketch, etc.).
- Have a plan—what do you want to do with yourself in a nonprofit organization?
- Have an agenda—know what is important to you.
- Serve on boards or otherwise volunteer with nonprofit organizations.
- Be prepared to change jobs in order to move up. Take risks with your career.
- Don't ignore people skills. Being a good accountant will not help you as much as being a good motivator of people."

Mid-Nonprofit-Career Doctoral Students

As I was completing this book I had the pleasure of teaching a class of doctoral students focusing their attention on the nonprofit sector. This national cross-section of doctoral students was recruited from various parts of the country by Bob Leduc (see p. 54). They are midcareer people for the most part.

I questioned them about their work and advice they might have for you. Here are a few selections. They suggest that you:

"Train about politics by finding an issue in which you really believe . . . you will find out about power structures, meet people who can help you in your field, and over time sophisticate your ability to deal with people with whom you disagree."

> *Larry Amerose*
> *Division Director of Community Relations*
> *Auraria Higher Education Center*
> *Denver, Colo.*

Develop technical skills. "As the field becomes more technical, I believe education specific to the field is more important."

Develop a very strong commitment to your work. "Commitment continues to be the most important single attribute of the (successful) employees in the field."

Mike Ostrowski
Executive Director
Family and Children Service of Midland Inc.
Midland, Mich.

"Know that you possess the capacity to work in an environment that requires flexibility, imagination and stamina."

"Assess the specific skills you bring to the sector and be willing to apply them and increase them through formal education and training."

Louise R. Iennaccaro
Executive Director
Center for Management Assistance
Kansas City, Mo.

"Be prepared to explore and test every value you have."

Anonymous

"Know your value system and be as well schooled as you can be. At a minimum, spend as much time thinking as doing. Never be afraid of mistakes and change direction as soon as you know you are wrong." "Build a good support system but don't inordinately fear individual action.

Allen Oliver
Executive Director
Delaware Guidance Service
Wilmington, Dela.

"Develop a good understanding of organizations and systems and how they function and change. If you aren't interested in changing the system, get out now because you'll do more harm than good."

Jack Wolf
Professor
University of Manitoba

"Become familiar with the liberal arts to broaden your creative spirit. Be a risk-taker. Don't shy away from asking questions and making assertions. Develop listening and analytical skills. View things, data and people from an ecological or holistic perspective."

> *Al Kelly*
> *Executive Director*
> *San Luis Valley Area Health Education Center*
> *Alamosa, Colo.*

"Be prepared to work harder and longer than you ever dreamed possible."

> *Anonymous*

"Be prepared for some negative reaction to your lack of profit motive and some quizzical admiration of your choice, too. You can find opportunities to 'stretch' yourself almost daily."

> *Lisa Kaichen*
> *Executive Director*
> *Childrens Charter of the Courts of Michigan, Inc.*
> *Lansing, Mich.*

"Keep your sense of humor. Don't offend people with style when you can offend them with substance." "Don't be afraid to risk— failure is the best opportunity for growth."

> *Charlie Allinson*
> *Executive Director*
> *Developmental Disabilities Council*
> *Region 10*
> *Delta, Colo.*

There are a number of common themes that appear frequently in these vignettes about a few of my friends and colleagues. I'd like to call several of them to your attention.

- *Try to become clear about your own values.* Most mental health improvement activities, from the intensively professional to the most laid back self help, seem to get around to the "be true to yourself" notion sooner or later. This sector, in the main, honors clearly articulated values.
- *Keep beefing up your skills.* The formal education people call it life long learning. But everyone can aspire to be a scholar, a reader, a thinker, an analyzer. Try to stimulate that part of you that nurtures your curiosity.

And, don't scatter these efforts. Aspire to be some kind of a T-shaped person. This concept, was adopted and adapted from my days of training management consultants at McKinsey & Company, the finest management consulting firm in the world, in my judgment.

The idea is fairly simple. In order for an individual to be successful, one needs both a variety of more "generalist" and management/administrative skills, *plus* deeper skills and experience in both a management/administrative area *as well as* at least one program focus. See the schematic layout below for an illustration of the concept:

Fig. 4-1: The T-shaped person – a schematic illustration

Management/ Administrative Skills:	Finance	Program Design	Human Resource Management
Program Focus	Health Care Delivery		Nonprofit Theatre

Management/Administrative Skills ⟶   FUND RAISING   HIGHER EDUCATION   ⟵ Program Focus

Don't panic! You don't have to start with a wide horizontal T-bar or a very deep spike. Each job and forward step in your career can add depth and/or breadth to your "T."

- *Don't be afraid to try something . . . especially something new!* Are you the "only one" who is scared? No way! Each of the people I interviewed, most of whom I have known for years, have experienced the full measure of the normal anxiety and stress that one naturally feels when thinking about and then executing a major change.

- *Ask others for help, clearly . . . and help others whenever you can.* We all need guidance, a fresh idea, a supportive listener or some other form of tender loving care (TLC) from time to time. Like the two dimes you "borrow" to make a call, pass on to someone else later the care and concern some generous soul gives to you. One of the joys you will rediscover is how much pleasure the giver gets from the gift well given!

Here is the proof of the pudding. Since I began these interviews less than a year ago, the following career changes have taken place:

- *Phyllis Quan* has struck out fully on her own as the president of her own fund raising consulting firm in San Diego. She'll do very well—she has an excellent and well-earned reputation.

- *Joan Welsh* has accepted a new management position as the California Program Director for the Pacific Crest Outward Bound School based in Santa Monica, California. As a Trustee of the Pacific Crest Outward Bound School, I played a small part in identifying and recruiting Joan for this position. The message in this point is that we *all* have an obligation and an opportunity to help talented people stretch and grow in their nonprofit careers.

- *Arthur Himmelman* has left the warm and safe world of foundation management to tackle an exciting and very stimulating project focused on better understanding of public-private partnerships.

- *Bob Leduc* has also left foundation work to concentrate on his leadership position at INPOM, including a special assignment as the president of the Visiting Nurses Associations of America, and complete his doctorate degree in nonprofit management at the University of Colorado at Denver.

Even when you are 'in the pits' with your own career search, it may do you as much good as the recipient to help someone else along in their search.

* * *

Explore these career stories again . . . and read between the lines. These people worked hard for their progress. They have an additional common thread—they care! My daughter Wyeth goes to a Quaker high school, Friends Seminary in New York City. I have learned through Wyeth and the Quaker spirit of her school to look carefully for the many good things in every person. It isn't easy in the middle of a career change or search, but start with the most critical element: you!

After that, seek out others who are already dedicated laborers in the nonprofit vineyard. I'm confident that you will find, as I have, inspiration in exploring the work of others in nonprofit organizations: how they got into the sector, why they came, what they do, why they stay, and where they hope to go with their career in the nonprofit sector. You will find that the bulk of them are: Doing Well by Doing Good!

PART II

HOW TO FIND THE RIGHT NONPROFIT JOB FOR YOU

FORTY-TWO ACTION STEPS FOR SEEKING NPO JOBS

This chapter will explore over forty specific actions you can take if you wish to secure a job in the nonprofit sector. As far as this writer knows, any person who has systematically taken these actions has secured a position in due course. But before you begin, be sure your motivation to change positions or careers is high enough to sustain you through the process. As Richard Bolles, the well-known author, recently indicated, one should think of job hunting as another full-time job in itself. Then, "if the vision sounds like too much work, you're not ready."[1] A summary listing of the action steps appears at the end of the chapter.

STRATEGIES FOR RESEARCH

Before you launch your job search, take some time to assess your talents and skills and make more explicit your values and preferences (see part I). The key to this activity is to begin to develop a clear picture of that unique package of skills, experience, and abilities that is *you!* Take a look at some questions such as: are you an administrator or an analyst, a problem solver or a problem definer, or do you want to be able to use a wide variety of skills and talents in one position? How effective a communicator are you with people at all levels in an organizational hierarchy? Do you prefer a lot of people contact or a "solo practice?" Do you work well with a team? How do you handle supervision—both giving and receiving? How much social content must your own work contain? How much pressure and stress is acceptable to you?

You should also begin to think early on about what kinds of settings you would ideally want to work in: large or small; a provider of services or grant giver; in operational jobs such as the direct provision of services to people—or one step removed from direct service in management, administration, or planning; lots of numbers and paper or lots of people and noise? With a global, national or local focus? Is it important to have fancy, nice, or spartan surroundings— or do you care? You spend the majority of your waking hours working, getting to and from work, and eating—it might as well please and stimulate you as much as possible.

These are just a few thought-starter questions. The key is to sort through *all* the questions *you* have—and then spend some time with yourself sorting out the answers that speak best to you.

If you are having trouble getting clear about your skills, talents, abilities, and interests buy Richard Bolles' *What Color is Your Parachute? A Practical Manual for Job Changers* in paperback. It is available in most bookstores or any library. It contains a number of helpful exercises to help you get started and focus your energies along constructive avenues. Another useful book is Robert Traxel's *Manager's Guide to Successful Job Hunting,* especially chapter 3, "The Product: All About You."

Now, to get underway I recommend that you get out *today* and talk to all kinds of people and:

1. Start with who you really are.

Now we are not talking about a long meandering voyage of self-discovery here—but I am going to ask you to take some critical time up front to sort out *and articulate* who you really are. There are a number of specific actions you could take to get underway. None of them are magical, but they will help, and only *you* can take them.

- Write down, *yes, write down*, statements using action verbs about your skills, talents, and accomplishments. Do it right now—at least five, or how about ten? Have you run out of things to write down? No problem, we all do. Go interview your friends, co-workers, or classmates. Ask your Aunt Minnie or your Uncle Fred about their views of your special skills, talents and accomplishments. Write down their responses. Then expand your list with those action verbs leading the way each time.
- *Expand* on why you have chosen to explore the nonprofit sector. If it's service to other people that "speaks to you," what kind of service?

  - Do you like the idea of advocating for someone else?

- Are you willing to help people "take on" powerful organizations, big bureaucracies, or whatever? Can you handle defeat and come back again? And again? And again?
- Do you enjoy hands-on helping? Can you do it eight hours a day? Five days a week?
- Do you like managing and administering others? Will that kind of work be too much like the headaches you have where you now work?
- Is it being near or around certain kinds of activities or people (dance or dancers; hospitals or doctors, nurses, patients) that appeals to you?
- Can you handle a heavy diet of people in trouble? Not everyone can. Be honest and skip certain kinds of direct service jobs if they aren't for you.

2. Have as clear a goal in mind as you can.

Write a few of them down to see how they look. Do they seem like you? Is it what you want to do? It's a good idea to have one or two *primary* job goals as well as a secondary or fallback job goal in mind as well.

You will get further in a job search if you are clear about where you want to go. If you are not clear, that's O.K. We can deal with that issue, and you won't be alone. Many of us "don't know what we want to be when we grow up," and the rest of us change our minds several times in the course of our work lives.

3. If you are already working and not happy just now, complete the job change worksheet.

For those of you who are currently employed, this exercise may help to ensure that you won't leave a fairly good situation for one that may not be as good without thinking the issues through quite carefully (see appendix E).

4. Get a good "workplace" from which to conduct your search.

If you are still employed you can use your office or place of work, but it will take discipline and discretion on your part. If you are not currently employed, you could work at home (I recommend setting up a separate, quiet place) or use or rent modest space elsewhere. Perhaps you have a friend or relative with a desk and phone in a quiet corner.

You will also need a telephone with an answering machine or service, typing equipment or a secretarial service, and access to your local library for research on nonprofit organizations. Your "search office" must be a serious place where you go to work. As you sit down in that place, get right to work. There isn't time for non job-related play or feeling sorry for yourself. Straighten out your desk drawers some weekend after you are employed happily—not now! If you stay on *this* job, you'll have another great one with pay in no time!

5. Start your search from your own strengths and contact network.

Here's how. Make a list of the first fifty people that you know well enough to write or call about potential jobs. We are not talking about your three best friends here. The fifty on the list just have to be people you can contact who might respond positively in some way to you and have just one constructive idea about the availability of any jobs you might enjoy . . . or contacts that might lead to a job!

This is hard to do, so you might start close to home by getting ideas from your current co-workers (if they know or should know that you are thinking about looking for a new position), your social friends (even though you may not think of them in work terms very often), former teachers and professors, friends of the family, and people you have met through work. Going from this point, here are some additional categories you might tap:

- Old college friends (who can be tracked down through alumni offices and bulletins or by going to any and all reunions or local meetings—you need to go and work those crowds!). Get your college and graduate school alumni address book today and start "dialing for dollars/contacts."
- Former co-workers and their friends and/or contacts.
- Family friends, including those you have not seen in a long time and those whose dinner party invitation you did not return. Perhaps even more important will be the contacts they may introduce to you.
- Relatives including the distant relations on the other side of the family with whom you haven't communicated in several years.

As luck would have it, your best job could come from the contact you hated making most! Who ever promised it was going to be always easy . . . or fair?

Start constructing this list immediately. *Complete it today; yes, today.* Tomorrow, draft a second list of fifty persons that you were reluctant to contact when you drew up the first fifty names. Your job probably will lie somewhere along the network that you are going to build in the second fifty contacts. Assuming this could be true (McAdam's Law), get to work on contacting the second fifty immediately also. You don't have to do it all at once. But you must set a goal—a minimum of three new contacts per day for openers.

Identify those individuals you want to tell about the skills you enjoy using most. Pick good listeners first. More specifically, start with people with whom you would be comfortable talking and who are likely to offer kind and helpful suggestions in return. Listen to them and if their advice, even if it is a bit critical, sounds right, clean up your act—and take it on the road *right now!*

If this task is quite difficult for you, remember that you won't have to do it too many times—and keep the lists of contacts in your files so if and when you have to do it again, you won't have to start building those lists of contacts from scratch.

I cannot emphasize enough how important it is to begin this process immediately, and to do it carefully and completely.

It may well be the single most important task in your job search. Peter Granovetter, in *Getting A Job: A Study of Contacts and Careers,* Harvard University Press, 1974, studied the job search techniques of a sample of more than 10,000 professionals. He found that approximately 65 percent obtained their jobs through contacts. A surprising percentage were *not* friends and relatives but either virtual strangers or friends of friends.[2]

If you have enough lead time, consider joining organizations in geographic or professional areas of interest to learn more about your field and make contacts. Always have some learning mission along with the desire to make contacts. It will make your efforts pay off on one of the goals nearly every time. Such "joining up" may even occasionally help you gain access to "inside" knowledge of job listings or advance notice of same. But, seldom is there as much "inside" as all of us out here "outside" think.

Don't be limited to your own city. Go statewide. Consider other nearby states, even international settings. A social science friend suggests that most people's contacts exist in small (fewer than 200 persons) and overlapping networks.

Potential connections can move back and forth through these networks, even across oceans, with the ease of a letter. So, let's keep those cards and letters coming and going!

6. Use your placement office.

If your university or graduate school has a placement office, use it! If you move away, try to get reciprocity with a local institution. If you didn't go to college, stop in and see if they might be willing to help you, just because you are a pleasant neighbor. You might be in a position one day to hire their graduates or make a contribution to the school.

You can maximize your results from placement office contacts by:

- Securing the appropriate registration materials in advance by telephone, mail, or dropping by during their office hours (call ahead to be sure they are open).
- Scheduling an appointment with the head of the placement office or the person who works most closely with employers. If it is a larger university, find out if there is one person most knowledgeable about your areas of interest. See that person if at all possible.
- Learning about how they process job leads, finding out, for example:

  - How often job opportunity lists are updated.
  - Whether you can secure list updates over the telephone.
  - Whether *you* must keep the placement office supplied with copies of your resume.
- Trying to build rapport with the placement office staff. If they take a personal interest in your search you can get considerably more leverage from your efforts.

7. Make it easy for people to help you.

Just as in your professional work you will want to structure recommendations or activities so that it is easy for your boss, your board, or a constituency to say, "yes," do the same in your job search. Think carefully about how each person you might ask for help might provide that help most effectively. Some people are more effective letter writers; others are more effective at making a phone call on your behalf. Whatever you ask someone to do, give them the tools to execute the task easily: the phone number, the address, a stamped, self-addressed envelope or whatever. You needn't carry this point to the extreme, but if you are very thorough, it will pay off! And, they will remember *you*, the one that was so very well organized and thoroughly prepared. You made it particularly easy for them to say, "yes"!

If the person won't do what you requested, have a fallback request prepared. Try to ask for some action, even if it's a referral to another interviewer, of each person you see. You are selling yourself—and you need to close the sale! You won't be able to do so every time, so maximize the opportunities! Keep building your contact lists and networks!

8. Do careful and extensive research on both the segments and the specific organizations of the nonprofit sector in which you are interested.

If you don't know much about the nonprofit sector, reread the balance of this book (especially chapters 1 through 4 and 8) carefully before you go much further here. They will give you an overview of the sector, tell you what the work is like, and talk about key future issues and how they may affect work in the sector.

A good source for general background information about the sector and the organizations in it are people in your geographical area who now work for NPOs. And, since NPOs are everywhere, there are nonprofits very close to your home or workplace right now. You could become acquainted with a local NPO by calling on the executive director or personnel director of your local hospital, YWCA, YMCA, church or synagogue social service effort, or a local nonprofit theater, to name just a few. You also no doubt have friends who are serving on the boards of nonprofit organizations—a local private school, a settlement house, or a shelter for battered women and children.

Current nonprofit sector workers or volunteers can help you begin to know the territory you are about to explore in depth and then master. They can also help you begin to build a network of people who will take varying degrees of interest (some providing assistance from time to time) in your search for a position and career in NPOs.

Start with the types of organizations that match most closely your assessment of your talents, skills, values, and preferences. Find out what types of positions they offer and the responsibilities involved (e.g., program associate in a foundation, policy analyst in a nonprofit planning agency, program administrator in a social services agency, or clerical worker in a hospital). Consider conducting exploratory interviews with a few of your key contacts as part of this research effort. Some of these contacts can provide you with information on a field or skill needed—but don't overdo this approach. As soon as you are ready, start the real job search—but not until then.

Here are a few concrete suggestions for sources that will identify additional nonprofit organizations you might contact to learn more about the sector.

- *Your local library.* The library, especially the reference and research sections, contains a wealth of information about the nonprofit sector in general and the specific nonprofit organizations that operate in your area. Appendix F contains lists of books, articles, and other documents about the sector and job hunting in it. Many of them are available in your local branch library. And if not, most smaller libraries have interlibrary loan arrangements that enable you to borrow books from the larger research libraries in nearby towns or cities.

    Don't be afraid to ask your librarian for assistance. These folks are often very knowledgeable about their own resources and others available in the community.

- *College or university libraries.* If you find your local library isn't meeting all your needs, try the nearest college or university library. You may not be able to get lending privileges, but a brief self-introduction to the desk person or head librarian will almost always at least get you access to their stacks and reference rooms.

    Moreover, for those of you who have narrowed down your interests to the health care or the arts segments of the nonprofit sector, for example, there is an extensive professional literature about the work of individuals in health, law, medicine, and so on for most fields, as well as extensive materials on the sector segment (e.g., the arts) itself.

- *General directories.* There are a variety of directories that can be useful to you, starting with *Guide to American Directories,* a directory of directories. It contains "a listing and description of 6,000 directories with over 300 major industrial, professional, and mercantile classifications. Useful in locating membership names and titles."[3] In a number of communities there may also be a directory of all the organizations within many of the subsegments, such as health (a directory of hospitals and clinics in your area) or the arts (a directory of theaters or a listing of cultural organizations in your county or state).

- *Specialized directories.* In this information-packed society of ours, there are a number of other interesting directories and guides to the various fascinating segments of the nonprofit sector. Among them are:

  Directory of Executive Recruiters. A cross-indexed listing of over 2,300 recruiter offices in the United States, Canada, and Mexico.

  The College Placement Annual. A directory in which employers seeking to recruit people spell out their interests. Although very few nonprofit employers use this approach, corporations, large government units, and other organizations with positions similar to those you may be seeking in the nonprofit sector may be listed here.

  The Encyclopedia of Associations. A listing, by field, of groups of professionals and others in many areas of interest.

  A Guide to Professional Development Opportunities for College and University Administrators: Seminars, Workshops, Conferences, Institutes and Internships.

  Occupational Outlook Handbook. An assessment of job outlooks prepared by the U.S. government; available in most good reference libraries.

- *Units of governments.* Since all levels of government provide money to nonprofit organizations in purchase-of-service agreements or other types of contracts, they are a good source of information. Also, your state (and some local) government probably has a charities registration section with information on a variety of nonprofit organizations. They also are likely to have names, addresses, telephone numbers, names of the members of the board of directors, budget sizes, and descriptions of basic services. The attorney general's office in many states is another good source.

- *Form 990s.* All nonprofit organizations with budgets over a minimum size must file forms with the Internal Revenue Service. These forms contain a considerable amount of information about the organization, its leadership, and its finances.

- *The Internal Revenue Service Code.* Published by Prentice-Hall; section 501 contains detailed definitions of the various types of nonprofit organizations.

71

- *The Grants Index of the Foundation Center.* The Grants Index is available at the main office of the Foundation Center[4] or at any one of the regional collections. (The locations of these collections also can be obtained from the main office.)

    These listings in the Grants Index, which are organized topically, will help you to identify NPOs in your area of interest that have received grants for various purposes.

Any of the directories cited above can be a useful place to browse in the early days of your search while you are still sorting out those aspects of the sector in which you would most like to work. And, there are more useful sources below.

- *The Yellow Pages* of the local telephone directory.

- *Associations of organizations and/or individuals within specific segments of the nonprofit sector.* There are many different organizations with a wealth of information about specific segments of the nonprofit sector. The modest listing of these organizations with their addresses found in appendix G will get you started on one or two trails which will be useful to you. Practice being a good tracker to follow this resource trail to the end—your new job! I have organized the list by a few basic categories. Your local research librarian could help you expand the list further.

- *Job banks.* There are a number of specialized job or talent banks that may contain leads on specific positions in nonprofit organizations. Although many of them have been set up with a focus on mainstream for-profit sector positions, they also have other positions in government and nonprofit work.

    Some of the organizations you might contact include, for example:
    - The Urban Coalition (national)
    - National Organization for Women (national)
    - Catalyst (for women in New York City)

- *Unions.* A number of unions are focused on industry segments within the nonprofit sector. Contact a local union office in your locale and ask for their information officer or director of research. If they are a small local, ask for the name and telephone number of such a person in their national organization.

- *Lobbyists.* If you are located in or near your state or the nation's capital you might contact the government unit that registers lobbyists in the area. Identify lobbyists who work in program areas or issues of interest to you. Contact a few of them for suggestions regarding nonprofit organizations that seem to be (a) growing, (b) out in front on key issues, and (c) attempting to provide leadership on key issues or in program development.

- *Annual reports of foundations.* Nearly all well-managed foundations publish annual reports or lists of grantees (organizations that receive their grants). These are usually available by:
  - Writing or calling the foundation; you can get a list of the major foundations in such directories as *The Taft Foundation Reporter,* or *The Taft Corporate Giving Directory,* available from my publishers or your library (see also Appendix F).
  - Visiting the regional or cooperating collections of the Foundation Center.

- *Writers about the nonprofit sector.* Among the most knowledgeable individuals about the sector or one of its segments are the people who either earn their living following it—or who find it sufficiently fascinating to devote countless hours of personal time to studying how it works and then writing about it. For example, two of the most knowledgeable newspaper people are David Johnston of the Los Angeles Times and Kathleen Teltsch of the New York Times. Many of the book and journal writers are cited elsewhere in this book; see the Notes at the end of each chapter and Appendix F. Find others by digging through the periodic literature, newspapers, journals, and books. Then write them a letter, call, or ask to see them. Most writers are not asked for direct advice very often. If your letter is inviting, brief, and clear, you may make a good contact . . . but don't assume that they will have time to answer.

- *Other local sources.* There are a number of other useful sources in your geographic area that may help you to identify and research nonprofit organizations. These include:
  - Consultants to nonprofit organizations (see your Yellow Pages or section publications)
  - Community service organizations such as the Elks, Lions, Rotary, Kiwanis, Optimists, Masons, or Shriners
  - Regional health planning bodies

- Local religious organizations
- Chambers of Commerce
- Welcome-wagon or other location/relocation groups
- Real estate people
- Local bankers
- Travel agencies
- Local economic development groups
- Personnel departments of large employers in the area
- Key volunteer or "charity people" known in your community for their support of NPOs.

STRATEGIES TO GET YOUR FOOT IN THE DOOR

9. Use a variety of approaches for each potential position.

One doesn't build a house with a single brick. The same is true for your job search. Many different approaches can be effective. Cover your bets by putting a number of different approaches to work for you. Your next job may be located in any number of different places. You may need to use a number of alternate approaches to find it.

The research on job hunting shows clearly that most jobs are found through personal connections built through a network of people. We have discussed how to do this elsewhere in this book. However, a number of people have found good positions through ads in newspapers, direct "cold calls" on nonprofit organizations, by reading daily municipal, state and federal bulletins on large contracts being let (new jobs follow new money many times), researching the annual reports of nonprofit organizations, attending job fairs, joining professional associations of people who work in their area of interest, visiting graduate placement offices of universities, and so on.

Try a variety of approaches, but don't get spread too thinly.

10. Do some volunteer work.

Nonprofit organizations are among the most prodigious users of volunteers. It is not too difficult to land a volunteer position. Such work will give you firsthand experience with the sector, its inhabitants, and the kind of activities that go on in a particular NPO as well as in that segment of the sector. It also builds and broadens your contact network.

There are many ways to contact nonprofit organizations about possible volunteer positions. Here are a few samples just to get you started.

- Direct contact; just call or make an appointment to visit them in person.
- Columns in your local newspaper on public service opportunities (e.g., the *Los Angeles Times* often runs listings of volunteer opportunities and features articles fairly frequently by writers such as David Johnston on the nonprofit sector.
- Mayors' offices of volunteers.
- Voluntary action centers.
- Churches and synagogues.
- Religious philanthropies and social action groups such as Catholic Charities (in most cities), Jewish Fund for Justice (Washington, D.C.), United Church of Christ (many cities), American Friends Service Committee (the Quakers, in many cities), and many more.
- Hospital volunteer organizations.
- Public agencies such as planning or budget sections, community boards and commissions.
- Public officials' offices.
- Service clubs or fraternal organizations.
- Local business groups or chambers of commerce.
- "Good government" groups.

11. Develop a mentor (or two).

Mentors can play a very important role in developing or changing one's career. As a generally senior, more knowledgeable, and potentially powerful advocate for you, a mentor can be enormously helpful. If you can develop such a relationship with a mentor in a key nonprofit-relevant position, he or she can help you open doors, plan your job search strategy, and solve problems along the way.

The mentor relationship is described at some length in Daniel D. Levinson's book, *The Seasons of a Man's Life*. In it, Levinson points out that the mentor is generally several (or more) years older, and can be found in the workplace or be a friend or relative. "The term 'mentor' is generally used . . . to mean teacher, adviser or sponsor."[5] Mentoring is defined not in terms of formal roles but in terms of the character and the relationship and the functions it serves.

Levinson identifies these roles that mentors can play. Each one may only play a few of them—very few play them all:

- teacher
- sponsor
- host
- guide
- exemplar
- supporter and facilitator of the realization of one's career and personal "dream."

Most of these functions should be transitional in nature, coming to an end at some point in time.

It may be possible in the nonprofit sector to identify a mentor or quasi-mentor who might be willing more readily to play at least the role of your sponsor. The nonprofit sector is chronically short of new, highly talented, motivated people. In your search you may be able to locate and forge a bond with someone who takes such an interest in seeing you work in a productive role in the sector that he or she sponsors and facilitates your search. Good hunting!

If you are unable to identify and connect with a mentor during this search, try to develop one or two during your next job tenure. They not only can facilitate your growth in your immediate position but also can help you move constructively should such an action seem appropriate.

12. Develop one or two good resumes—but don't overconcern yourself with them.

Of greater importance is to polish your cover letter. Make the cover letter sharp and to the point. Show how you would be valuable to the organization.

If you develop two resumes, emphasize different aspects of your skills and what you have done. *Use action verbs*. Write it *briefly*. Use simple language and assume it will be read by lay persons unfamiliar with jargon. Put your background and experience in the best possible light; type it neatly; proof it *very* carefully (typos suggest carelessness and misspelled words are even worse); and *always* carry several copies with you wherever you go—even on weekends.

Don't worry about your past. You can't change it, although you can present yourself in a positive, straightforward light. *And worry as little as possible; focus your energy on your future actions.*

Don't let this aspect of your search cause you anxiety. The main value of your resume is to get you in the door, face-to-face with someone who might have a job.

If you are having trouble with your resume, use a standard outline from one of the existing books on resume preparation. As part of your preparation for the writeup:

- Make a list of the best and perhaps happiest things you have done. Write down the ten that best illustrate the types of accomplishments you would like to continue to have. Don't be afraid to emphasize actions that suggest or document your capacity for leadership roles of any kind. The sector particularly needs motivated, caring, and capable leaders at all levels.
- Take the five or six that have seemed most valuable to your past employers (or that you guess will interest a future one). Write them again, this time using *action words* that define best what you did. Boil them down to as few words as possible without losing or changing the essence of the idea. Make sure all other descriptions of what you did anywhere in your resume or cover letters are also action oriented and of similar quality to the key five or six.
- Be prepared to redraft and edit your resume four or five times. Ask a colleague who writes well to go over it carefully and to critique it thoroughly.
- Proofread it *very* carefully! Triple check your telephone number and address. Prospective employers will conclude you are a sloppy thinker if your materials have errors.
- Prepare a first-rate cover letter. It is as important as the resume itself, even more important. Space it well. Keep it short, simple, and clear. Tell the reader who you are, identify your most important accomplishments (especially if they are memorable), and then highlight several more. Your goal is to motivate the reader to read your full resume. And, more important, to make an appointment to see you!
- If you want your application for the position treated confidentially, clearly indicate this and provide the address and telephone numbers to which you want communication directed.

13. Conduct your search in a well-organized fashion and be systematic.

Use a simple, easy-to-maintain system to which you will remain committed throughout your search. Stick with it *religiously*! Record, file, and retrieve in the same way all the time. Use a five by seven card for each contact; or, use some other simple recording and filing system, such as a manilla folder for each nonprofit organization in which you are interested. Record the name, title, telephone number, address and zip code, what type of contact you had with staff, when they responded, and what follow-up you have done, including dates. See figure 5-1 at right.

Record a personal note or two on each person to refresh your memory about them in case you have an opportunity for future contacts. Jot down their secretary's or receptionist's name, too. Making a cheerful, friendly impression on the interviewer's secretary can be very helpful, and, on occasion, critical to your search. For example, Ms. Marge Balapole and Ms. Jean Van Sickle in our foundation's offices are vital members of our office team. What they think is important . . . and it counts!

Do a cross-reference on each card so you know through which network you reached this person. On separate sheets, keep a list of each network you build and the people who help you start each one. *Also be sure to remember them with a written thank-you note.*

14. Review professional journals and the major newspapers (in acceptable geographic locations) carefully and religiously.

Spend a little time in the library to become familiar with the periodical literature in the nonprofit subsegment in which you have the most interest. You will be (and sound) very well informed when asked, "what kinds of journals and other things do you read?"

Turning to the newspapers, please be aware that some ads only appear once. Read every day. Pay attention to the nonprofit organizations receiving major grants or expanded government funds. They may have openings.

15. Construct a job search resource binder.

Most of us who write in the job/career search area suggest some kind of organizing device such as a Job Search Resource Binder. There is no magic in any of the approaches. Frankly, how carefully and well you prepare any reasonable organizing tool matters more than which one you use. If you don't already have one in mind, appendix H provides one format that you can adapt to your particular needs. The key here, friends, is to do it carefully and accurately. Keep it up to date!

Figure 5-1: An interview record card (front side)

(NPO Name) _____

(Interviewer's Name) _____ (Telephone) _____

(Address) _____ (Secretary's name) ____

(Address) _____

Comments from initial call: _____

_____

_____

Follow-up comments: _____

_____

_____

_____

Referred by: _____

_____

Figure 5-1: An interview record card (back side)

Other persons to whom referred:

Name _____

(Telephone)

Name _____

(Telephone)

Background information on NPO: _____

Directions to organization: _____

16. Consider getting involved in a local or regional political campaign.

You will probably be able to make a serious and substantive contribution if you care to do so, and you may have an opportunity to demonstrate and/or polish some of your communication skills as well as make some helpful contacts. Many people interested in politics are also interested in nonprofit organizations working on issues that concern them. Hence, you can make some more of those critical contacts.

17. Consider taking a course in nonprofit organization management at a local college or university, if available.

In New York City and elsewhere I'll wager, it is claimed that some of the evening courses at the local universities such as New York University or the New School for Social Research are far better places to meet interesting unattached men or women than local singles bars. It's true! But beyond finding Mr./Ms. "Right," you may find that a quality local course on nonprofit organization management or a survey course on the nonprofit sector can:

- Provide you with useful information about the sector and specific organizations in it, including the jargon as well as some notions about the key values and concepts.
- Acquaint you with classmates who are already working for NPOs.
- Expose you to the instructor who may well be a senior person in a nonprofit organization. But don't get your hopes up too much here. These are busy folks who teach "on the side" for the pleasure of it. They may not be able to take very much time on your job search. On the other hand, you may be just the person they are looking for. I always review the students I have taught in evening courses when I am thinking about a new hire. Unfortunately for job seekers we are going to be a modestly staffed foundation (lean and . . .) always.

18. Use a simple calendar to plan each week of your search.

Set measurable goals to be accomplished each day, each week, and each month. Write them down in your calendar. You can use a simple daily calendar purchased in a stationery store, or even a lined spiral binder about one-half to two-thirds the size of a standard sheet of paper. Use this calendar to help plan, organize, and program your activities right up until that celebration dinner after a successful month on your new job!

Here is one approach—modify it, make it yours, but pick one and do it EVERY DAY! You may find it useful to arrange your daily calendar sheets as in figure 5-2 on pages 84 and 85.

The date and the appointments, including scheduling a group of calls you need to make at a time when you are most likely to reach persons (i.e., 9:30—11:30 a.m. and 2:30—4:00 p.m., *in their time zones*) are fairly self-explanatory. Don't be bashful about asking for directions to the interviewer's office (you can always call the receptionist or secretary later if you are concerned about taking the interviewer's time). Or you can get a map and plan your route and where to park (or how to get there via public transit) well in advance. Don't over-schedule appointments. Two to three appointments is the maximum for a full day unless they are very routine exploratory visits. Leave plenty of time for the unexpected!

The goals for the week should be part of a larger "master plan." This "master plan" should be thought out and initially drafted at the beginning of your job search. You will want to set timetables for yourself (recognizing that you will need to replan once you get into the search a bit). Although I cannot provide all of the major steps you will want to take to launch, carry out, and conclude successfully your search, the major ones are summarized in figure 5-3 on page 86. Work them onto a "master plan" calendar, a bit faster if you are looking full time, more slowly if you are working full time while you look.

The following paragraphs expand a bit on the suggested steps, a few of which were illustrated above. But, be sure to make them your own. It will be *how* you execute them that counts as much, if not more, than which steps you take. Here are a few particularly good ones:

A. *Establish specific, personal goals:* a long-term one—five to ten years (the kind of position you'd like to hold about that many years out); an interim one (the kind of position you think you'd like now); and short-term ones (the basic actions you must complete *right now* to get that position). A useful way to phrase each of these goals is to start each one with *action* words indicating something you are going to do. For example: My short term goals for this week are (1) *to mail* fifteen letters with my resume to health-care providers in Chicago,

(2) *to arrange* three interviews by Friday, and (3) *to contact* five new people who may have some additional job leads.

B. *Start with (or develop) a positive attitude (yes, you can do it) . . . and hold on to it!* Additional suggestions are made elsewhere in this chapter to help you if you need more assistance on strengthening your attitude about career search work.

C. *Pick some initial job (or what you want to do) targets.* If you are at a total loss here, get into Bolles' *What Color is Your Parachute* book, especially chapter 5, "Only You Can Decide: What Do You Want to Do?" If you feel you face more serious problems in this area see the material on counseling and other resources later in his book.

D. *Set a geographic focus.* This gives you a territory to start in, but don't lock in too tightly. Unless you just *have* to get back to Manhattan or Cucamonga, stay loose while you focus on Somewhere, USA.

E. *Make your first list of potential contacts.* See action number 5 earlier in this chapter.

F. *Make x number of calls/write y number of letters* (this week).

G. *Conduct z interviews* (this week).

H. *Send thank-you letters* (every time, yes, every time—even if you felt the contact or the interview was a total bomb. In fact, it is particularly important if you felt the interview did not go very well.

I. *Follow up,* but give them some time. Ask while you are there if they have established a timetable for a hiring decision.

J. *Select which offer to take.* See action number 39. You may not get to this step in the early weeks, but you *will* get there!

By the way, the computer jargon for this whole process is "iterative." You will repeat all or many of the steps several times—a few of them many many times. Just keep moving! One step at a time.

Review your progress frequently and write down what you are going to do to overcome any obstacles you feel you have encountered. Many of your tasks can be planned out well ahead of time. Set aside enough time in the days ahead to handle these tasks, to do followup, and to review your progress.

Be prepared for a job search that may take a number of months. More senior positions in popular cities can take nine to twelve months, and even longer, to land. And there is nothing wrong with you should it take a while.

Figure 5-2: A planning calendar page

Appointments			
Time	Person/Place	Address	Telephone
AM			
Noon			
PM			

Date _____

Goals for Week:

1.

2.

3.

4.

Key Actions to Do Today

1.

2.

3.

4.

5.

6.

7.

8.

9.

10.

**Expense
Record
Amount   Purpose**

Figure 5-3: Selected key steps in the job search

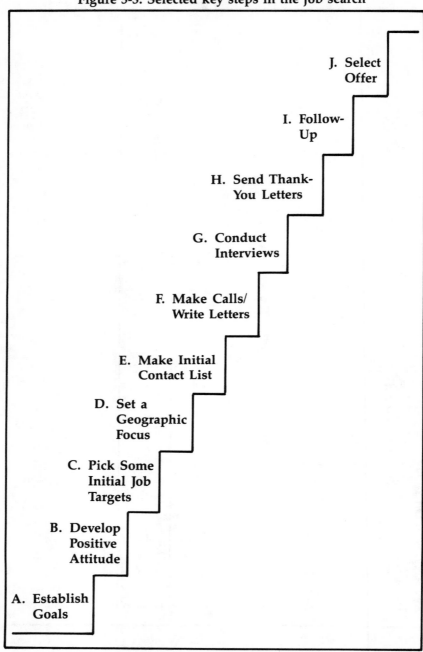

J. Select
Offer

I. Follow-
Up

H. Send Thank-
You Letters

G. Conduct
Interviews

F. Make Calls/
Write Letters

E. Make Initial
Contact List

D. Set a
Geographic
Focus

C. Pick Some
Initial Job
Targets

B. Develop
Positive
Attitude

A. Establish
Goals

19. Do something every day.

It will get you started. It will keep you going. It will expand your network. It will result in a job. It will help you avoid some of the normal depression everyone experiences when seeking work. *Keep moving! Keep acting!* Don't stop until you have been working in your new position happily for one month! Then smile . . . and recommend this book to three friends!

If you aren't currently working, consider presenting yourself as available for short-run consulting assignments, part-time work, or substantial volunteer duty. It can open up some new ideas and networks. It will keep your working "muscles" in tone. But, be sure the work has the potential to lead to something else, if at all possible. Also, reserve some personal and recreational time. A *little* time off will help you keep a sense of humor. But save the more serious indulging of yourself for after you have been employed for nine to ten months. Then you can take the vacation you deserve!

Ask your family and friends to remain supportive of your need to keep at this business of seeking a job *full time*. You should be able to continue to carry your share of non -ob-related responsibilities and tasks— but after hours, just as when you were employed in your last job.

20. Give priority to those actions that seem to have the most potential for getting you a job.

It will be terribly tempting many times during the job-seeking process to reorganize your desk, clean your apartment or house, or tackle some other low priority task. As you look at the tasks for the day, do the ones most likely to pay off vis-à-vis getting a job first. Then do one fun thing as a reward. Then get back to the work of looking for a job—there will be plenty of time for play later when you are happily employed.

STRATEGIES FOR THE INTERVIEW

21. Make the interview work for you.

Let the interviewer see you at your best! Let's not kid ourselves. Interviewing can make one nervous, whether you are the interviewer or the interviewee. Almost all of the job-hunting books around are filled with do's and don'ts about interviewing. I will provide you with my favorites. But first remember two things:

- The interviewers are also a little nervous. If they are scaring the daylights out of you, try to imagine them getting up in the morning without clothes on, with water pouring on their heads, or brushing their teeth with a mop—anything to regain your everyday sense of humor and priorities. Remember that they are human beings, just like you!
- Getting a job in the nonprofit sector that will contribute to making the world just a little bit better in some way is why you are doing this. It's an honorable and reasonable goal. Others with less talent and experience than you are already doing it. You *can* do it. Go for it!

Now, a few selected do's:

Do dress nicely (too conservative is better than too casual). Wear clean clothes, have hair cut or done neatly, a clean shave (or well-trimmed beard), shoes shined, nails trim and clean, and modest (if any) makeup. Note to reader: Pick from the above list according to your taste . . . and the "you" that will be hired (and thus must show up every day mostly as you present yourself). Wear something you also feel comfortable in—break in the new shoes two days before the interview.

Do arrive on time (not out of breath from running because you were late). This means getting up early, leaving time for a late bus or a difficult-to-find office. Did you fill the car with gas and check the tires the night before? Do you have cash for parking? Have you an alternate plan if the garage is full? Do you know how to get there on public transit? Are your directions clear?

Do speak loudly and clearly enough to be heard.

Do listen *very* carefully.

Do put both feet on the ground or in another relaxed sitting position if necessary and don't change it too frequently. Maintain an open body stance with your arms down and hands in lap or holding your note pad. Sit slightly forward—you will look alert, energetic, and "with it!"

Do emphasize your successful projects, especially those that can be measured and understood readily.

Do be enthusiastic: sell yourself—no one else is going to do it!

Do develop plans for how you can and will strengthen any areas in which you are now relatively weak or lack experience.

Do point out that you value helping others; tailor your comments to the nature of the nonprofit organization for which you hope to be working.

Do provide some physical feedback by nodding affirmatively once in a while when you agree or understand something particularly well, and smile so the interviewer can know your friendly side.

Do look the interviewer in the eye as often as possible (you will seem particularly earnest and honest this way). However, you don't need to stare.

Do have a firm, earnest handshake. If you are nervous and have wet, sweaty palms, find a way to dry the handshaking one on a handkerchief or another part of your clothing without being too obvious about it. And, don't worry; we all get a little nervous, and many people, even experienced professional actors and speakers, get sweaty palms once in awhile.

Do give the interviewer plenty of time to talk. He or she just might conclude that you are particularly bright if you do.

And now a few selected *don'ts:*

Don't fidget, smoke (even if invited to do so), or play with your hair or nails. If you need some physical action to quell nervousness, find one the interviewer can't see.

Don't slouch or slump. Stay up, alert, and lean just slightly forward without overdoing it.

Don't chew gum or breath mints; instead, brush your teeth well, use a good mouthwash, and pass up those garlic and onion sandwiches on interview days.

Don't knock your prior employers or colleagues.

Don't get lured into discussions of sex, religion, or politics. Stay with the job (but keep your antennae tuned for a reasonable range of compatibility on some of these issues).

Don't have a drink at lunch during or before an interview. If the interviewer does, join him or her with juice or club soda. You don't need to explain; just pass up the drink for now and stay alert to the task at hand. If pressed on a drink, say you are training for a long hike, a marathon or an amateur triathalon. If pressed harder, indicate that having a drink is most enjoyable in the evenings (if it is) but that you want to focus on learning more about their organization.

Don't get into your personal problems or provide excessive information. It is fine to give a thoughtful brief answer and then pause, inviting the next question. If there are a few silences, don't always feel you are responsible to fill them. If the silence goes on far *too* long, then ask a question.

Don't introduce any negatives about yourself if at all possible. Put every statement you can into the positive.

Don't lose your temper or become irritated no matter how the interviewer behaves. Your goal is to win a job offer, not to win any debates.

Don't ask about compensation for any overtime. You can discuss work hours, pay, and benefits after you receive a solid offer.

Don't forget to write up notes and fill out your interview records. Several of the actions to come provide you with more information about these interview records.

Don't forget to write a thank-you letter. (See appendix I for a sample, but make your thank-you letter your own.)

22. Be prepared for every interview.

Do your homework assiduously. Research carefully every organization that you are going to visit. Know generally where they fall in their "industry." Read journal articles in the current issues about that field. Find out through the Grants Index in the regional collections of the Foundation Center[4] the names of the major grantmakers in that field. Have a few interview questions prepared in advance to break the ice if the interview doesn't flow smoothly in the beginning.

Carry two working (try them in advance) ball point pens and paper for notes plus several extra resumes. Keep a summary of places you have interviewed as well as organizations or people about which you would like to learn more. Any interview can present an unexpected opportunity to gather new information. Get your personal details pulled together before you are asked for them, including the names, addresses, and phone numbers of the schools you have attended, the names, addresses, and phone numbers of previous employers, including the same information for a supervisor who would be familiar with your work, personal references (did you ask their permission and prepare them for reference check calls?), your social security number, your salary history, other courses and training experiences, and so on.

It may be helpful to prepare a personal fact sheet as a simple way to keep much of the essential information organized and handy. See figure 5-4.

If you want information on how to prepare for an interview in more detail or have special problems such as a prior arrest or convic-

Figure 5-4: Personal fact sheet

Name _____   Soc. Sec. No. _____

Current
Address _____   Driver's Lic.
                                     No. _____

Telephone   (H) (___) _____   (W) (___) _____   Zip code _____

Educational Background

High School
Address _____   Telephone (___) _____

Attended from _____   to _____

College/University
Address _____   Telephone (___) _____

Attended from _____   to _____

Figure 5-4, continued

Address _____ Telephone ( ) _____

Attended from _____ to _____

Degree Awarded: _____ Month/Year Awarded _____

Additional Training/Courses

Name of Course _____

Given by _____

Address _____

Telephone ( ) _____

Name of Course _____

Given by _____

Address _____

Telephone ( ) _____

Name of Course _____

Given by _____

Address _____

_____

Telephone ( ) _____

Employment History _____

Name _____

Address _____

_____

Telephone ( ) _____

Supervisor/Reference _____

Employed from _____ to _____

Nature of work _____

_____

Name _____

Address _____

_____

Telephone ( ) _____

Figure 5-4, continued

Supervisor/Reference _____

Employed from _____ to _____

Nature of work _____

_____

_____

Name _____

Address _____ Telephone ( )

_____

_____

Other References:*

Name _____

Address _____ Telephone ( )

_____

_____

Name _____

Address _____ Telephone ( )

_____

_____

Name _____

Address _____ Telephone ( ) _____

_____

_____

*Note: Put only people who can be reached by prospective NPO employers during the day—that is when it is done.

Personal

Birthdate _____ Height _____ Weight _____

How long lived at current address? _____ years

Prior address (last two) _____

_____

_____

_____

List special talents (e.g., languages) _____

_____

List special hobbies and interests (when you aren't working) _____

_____

_____

List service organizations and clubs to which you belong: _____

_____

_____

tion record, see Wright's *Hardball Job Hunting Tactics* (see also "Further Reading" appendix F).

23. Follow Goldberg's Two Laws.*

First, try to see someone with at least potential hiring power. Note that this may *not* be the personnel department. Second, if you can't, see anyone who will see you. It may lead to something. And, a face-to-face interview is always the most attractive, for it will enable interaction and feedback to take place. I cannot emphasize strongly enough how important it is to keep plugging away, using a variety of tactics to get in to see people face-to-face. This is virtually the only way jobs are secured!

24. Do several practice interviews.

If it's been a very long time since you have been in an interview situation, or you have never done it, practice on one or two organizations in related fields in which you have less initial interest. Get your interviewing "sea legs" under you and become comfortable talking confidently and directly about two very important subjects: you and your career. If you have trouble getting interviews, try a call before office hours to connect you with a busy executive without the hurdle of a screener in the way.

After you complete each practice interview, make notes to yourself regarding the things you feel went particularly well and the things that should be dropped or changed significantly. Practice at home or with a friend so that you are more of an old hand when you are "on" for real.

25. Don't take affronts personally.

Getting a new job is tough work. Sometimes it is made tougher by interviewers who are insecure or don't know how to interview very well. Help them out. Keep your wits about you. Stay in constant mental touch with your accomplishments and the things you can do well. If rude questions are asked, have a positive, upbeat approach to answering them. We'll talk more about "hardball" questions later.

---

*Coined by Ms. Lisa Goldberg, a successful New York City-based foundation executive who used an earlier draft of some material for this book and had several useful suggestions.

Rude interviewers may view you as a reminder that they, too, might one day need to seek a new position. They may be saying to themselves, "What if I were you and you were I, oh, how frightened I might be." As a result, they may be unduly negative or rude. *Don't take it personally.*

Take a different approach. Think about job hunting in transaction terms; maximize your exposure by seeing as many people as possible. Even though this will result in more rejections vis-à-vis a job right now, this effort will also lead to a connection through which you may get a job in the end. Honest!

If you do get screened out early in the process, ask in a gentle but clear way, "Why?" Use this information in a constructive way, if you can, in the next go around. If it happens later in the interview process, it may just be more a matter of chemistry—something none of us can do much about.

26. Get prepared to deal with rejection.

Yes, you are likely to be rejected. And it usually hurts a little, sometimes a lot. With these rejections most people feel frustrated and angry. Some of us can become fearful and experience waves of panic, "I'll never get a good job! I'd better take just anything."

It is normal for you to experience short doses of these emotions. Keep from being isolated and remain in motion. If you do, you will experience these feelings far less often and be able to turn them into positive action more quickly.

Remember the message of the old German proverb, "Fate leads the willing, drags the unwilling, but they both go." Take the waiting in stride. There is a job (in fact, several jobs) out there for you. Your preparation and action are going to help luck and fate along in the process of helping you find just the job you need to start that new career.

27. Reach out for help if you need it.

There are job search support groups in a number of localities. Try your local newspaper's business section or Gale's *Encyclopedia of Associations*. For those over age forty (we are growing stronger in numbers every day!), there are also Forty-Plus Clubs in many locales. There are also many associations organized by sector segments (e.g., allied health professionals, physicians and surgeons, nurses). For examples, review the list given above in action number 8. In addition, Appendix

G – *A Directory of Nonprofit "Umbrella" Organizations*—provides a number of other potential sources of both information and possible assistance or referral.

A number of these actions will be treated in greater depth in the pages that follow. The key point is that you are looking for just one attractive job. It may exist in a variety of different places. You should try a variety of approaches to maximize your exposure to potential jobs or to the people who will lead to that job. Talk with your friends and people who have recently been through it. Don't ever give up!

28. Be tireless.

Be steady. Keep going. Don't stop until you have actually begun work and know that you like the position (and that it likes you). Keep expanding your network by calling and writing every possible (*and even improbable*) lead. Get in touch with long-lost friends, even old enemies (isn't it fortunate that most of us generally mellow with time?).

Expand your network of contacts as you go. Never leave anyone's office without trying to secure several leads or additional contacts. Write down every contact. Ask specifically for addresses and telephone numbers while you are there—it could save hours. If your interviewer seems rushed, ask if you could visit with a secretary for a moment to get the proper spelling of the names, correct titles, and how to reach them. Ask if you can use the interviewer's name when you are contacting individuals who might assist you.

Meet with people face-to-face whenever possible. (see Goldberg's laws [Action 23]). Something better almost always happens, and you learn more. Don't get anxious about obligations and debts you are creating by building up this network. You will be able to repay any debts you create later by helping others. Sensitively.

29. Treat this process as a full-time job.

Get up early every morning, take a shower, eat something, and be *at it* by 9:00 a.m. Work at it all day. Call and write new contacts each day. Don't stop working at your search until the end of the day. Call. Write. Research. Read. Call some more. Write some more. Do this and you will get interviews. Get interviews and you will get a job. Get a job and you will launch a career! Then you'll be *Doing Well by Doing Good*!

30. Be almost ruthless.

Use every contact you have. You will need help obtaining work only a few times in your lifetime. Develop your contacts steadily. Follow up. Don't be afraid to ask—remember that if you don't ask, you don't get.

If you need and want help, ask for it directly. Don't expect people to know you need their help unless you ask for it clearly, pleasantly, and confidently. Remember that you can help others later.

Use a variety of approaches to your job search. But put the most time and energy behind the one(s) that seem(s) to produce the most results. Cut your losses quickly on approaches that, after giving them a good try, seem extremely unlikely to help.

31. Be positive.

Portray confidence, even if you are frightened, anxious, and convinced that you won't find a job. Never say, "I can't," or think, "I'm not very good at . . . ." Think about what you have *done, the good things you have done!*

Review your list of the ten most important or impressive work tasks you have completed (and enjoyed doing). Be prepared to describe each one in your interviews with a sentence that begins with an *action* verb (e.g. I *planned*, I *expanded*, I *managed*, I *built*, I *prepared*, and so on)!

Practice ahead of time. It will take a little time to get it down fairly smooth. Weave these action-oriented descriptions into your answers to questions during interviews. This will help reinforce what your resume says. It will make you seem (as you are) a potentially very valuable employee.

Think positively, especially now. You have embarked on a very important sales campaign to sell the most important product in the world—you! Negative thinking can be your worst enemy. Be realistic but don't allow yourself to slow down and slump.

Execute Brooke's gambit. Do one little thing special and nice for yourself *each day* to help keep your spirits up.

Indicate by your style that you plan to work hard *and* be a team player. Indicate that you can and will help others who work with the organization.

Don't let the entire interview focus on *you*. Try to spend at least one- third to one-half of the time exploring, *in a meaningful and positive way,* the good works of the NPO at which you are interviewing. Celebrate its positive actions and results. Also, try to learn a little about the person who is interviewing you.

32. Let the professional search firms know of your availability if you are seeking a senior position.

While search firms (sometimes called headhunters) can occasionally be helpful to the job seeker, they are most often helpful to their clients—organizations with a position to be filled. But, leave no stone unturned; you are looking for just one job. Moreover, some headhunters are very sympathetic to talented people who want to work in the nonprofit sector and may help you along your path.

For example, Mr. Norman Clement, Korn/Ferry International, Los Angeles, CA; Mr. Gerald F. Corrigan, Russel Reynolds Associates, Inc., Los Angeles CA; Arnie Miller, Isaacson, Ford, Webb & Miller, Boston, MA; and Ms. Toni S. Smith, Spencer Stuart & Associates, Chicago, IL., are examples of the cadre of *both* knowledgeable (about nonprofits) and sensitively helpful people in the executive search field.

33. Treat every interviewer as a client.

Be prepared for the interview. Do your homework on the organization ahead of time. Read the organization's annual report and any of its other publications you can secure. Have a number of good questions prepared in advance. Here are several examples:

A. What types of responsibilities might I look forward to in three to five years if I am successful with this organization?
B. What resources will be available to me in meeting my responsibilities?
C. How well will my responsibility and authority levels mesh in this position?
D. How are the communication channels between us to be structured?
E. What criteria do you use to measure (1) the organization's success, (2) the performance of individuals in general, (3) success in the specific position I am to fill?
F. What are the major obstacles impeding the progress of this organization?

G. Can you expand on my opportunities to learn, grow, provide additional services, exercise leadership, and acquire additional responsibilities, experience, and skills?

H. What aspects of this organization and the work here give you (and your colleagues) the most satisfaction?[6]

Take notes, but be aware that there is some disagreement about this recommendation. Some alleged experts believe that some interviewers may be offended, feeling you are not giving them your undivided attention (though I would argue that it is a greater compliment to be sure you get correctly, and remember the key points made by the interviewer). In fact, I believe that people who don't take a few notes either have *perfect* memories or don't care enough about the content of the interview to want to remember key aspects of it. I'm told that a few interviewers believe that note taking is a sign of a poor memory. My opinion is that this view is a bit silly, but you may need to be sensitive to this possible attitude. One approach is to ask if the interviewer would mind if you jotted down a few of the key points covered during the interview.

Show some concern for the interviewer as an individual. Look for specific ways you might be of service to the part of the organization with which the interviewer is most concerned. Be prepared to be very specific about concrete things you can and will do to help this organization carry out its mission more effectively. This often requires both homework and thought in advance of the interview.

Don't be overly informal too quickly. Err to the conservative side of *your* range in speech, dress, and demeanor. But don't try to be what you aren't or you won't be happy in the job later.

34. Be prepared for the tough question.

But don't assume every interviewer will throw you one. Prepare constructive and positive answers in advance for the more difficult questions you might prefer not to answer (i.e., why did you leave your last position, why should we hire you, what are your weakest points, and so on). Be *honest* but positive. Practice answering the toughest ones with good steady eye contact. On application forms, put "will discuss in interview" rather than a negative answer to a question, and then have a flexible, rehearsed but accurate answer to that question.

One note of caution about rehearsing. Don't over-rely on it. Many times the questions don't come in exactly the form you expected. The key to preparation is to have the basic main points down well. You can fill in the appropriate shadings and details tailormade to the situation.

35. Be flexible and schedule more rather than less time for an interview or meeting.

Busy people can often run late or have unexpected interruptions. Be prepared to be flexible in the interview if it takes one or two unexpected turns. Be open to new ideas and opportunities for which you may not have planned (you don't have to "sign up" or take them, but keep a little loose).

STRATEGIES TO IMPROVE YOUR CHANCES

36. Remember to say thank you to every person who gives valuable time to help you in your job search.

A short note after the interview also helps remind them of you and your interest in a new position. This sounds like more drudgery now, but you will remember those who take the time to say thank you to you in the future.

37. Be prepared to "close the sale" on the job you want.

Explicitly state your interest in the position, indicate why you are interested (assuming that this is true), and articulate several specific ways in which you have much to contribute to this NPO. Indicate, assuming that it is true, that you have a personal commitment to the nature and focus of the work of the organization.

38. Be accessible by phone.

Have your telephone number(s) on your resume (address and zip code, too). Include a telephone number that won't be busy all the time and that can receive messages during extended office hours. If necessary, get a second line for teenagers, just during your search. Borrow an answering machine or consider a telephone answering service temporarily, if no one is going to be at that number regularly.

Don't be afraid to follow up in a week or two; it shows you are interested and alert. A follow-up letter can be a good reminder that you are still out there and interested even after some time has passed.

39. Assess offers carefully and systematically.

After you have received an offer, ("thank you very much, I'm honored to be invited to join your agency") think it over carefully ("I'd like to give this offer the serious consideration it deserves and get back to you in _____ days."). Then be systematic about comparing this offer to any others you may have received. One approach is to use a matrix with your options in a column on the left and the key characteristics on the right. See figure 5-5 below.

Note that only you can fill in the job characteristics. Start with those items most important to you. Be totally honest with yourself. No one else need see this matrix. You alone will live with the results.

Another approach is set forth in Traxel's *Manager's Guide to Successful Job Hunting,* in which he suggests a number of criteria against which you may assess those offers you wish to take seriously. To what degree will the position you are contemplating meet some of the criteria in this ideal partial listing? Will it, for example:

A. Create an atmosphere between you and your nonproft organization employer of mutual feelings of confidence, appreciation, and respect?
B. Reward you adequately in both financial and emotional terms (doing well by doing good)?
C. Offer satisfactory communication and understanding between you and your colleagues?
D. Make you feel "good," "needed," and proud of your work?
E. Give you the opportunity to utilize fully your skills, talents, education, and abilities?
F. Offer adequate and flexible benefits, which you understand and can use?
G. Provide sufficient growth potential and enough freedom to act responsibly within a clearly communicated yet flexible structure?
H. Be located in a geographic area that is acceptable to you?
I. Provide adequate, healthy, and cheerful work conditions?[7]
J. Enable you to have some flexibility on job hours and work patterns?

Figure 5-5: Job comparison matrix

Job Characteristics Option	Growth Opportunities	Interest Level of Work	Nature of People Relationships	Pay and Benefits	Work Surroundings and Location

40. Help others once you are working.

Remember how difficult it was to get appointments and to live with the frustrations of unanswered telephone calls and letters? Break this cycle by helping others—be supportive and friendly. Once you are working, take time to make personal referrals, write letters, and make calls for people seeking work. Spend twenty minutes with someone if you can possibly assist them.

Keep a file of people you might be able to help in the future so you can make prompt and useful referrals when the opportunity presents itself. Keep a few notes on the individuals you see so that later you can share accurate information on them.

Keep a "Jobs Available" folder so you can make concrete referrals to potential job seekers whenever possible. We need talented people in positions of responsibility in this sector. You can help!

41. Critique your job search performance in writing once you have been hired.

About a month after you start work, write a memo to yourself for the next time you conduct a search treating what was most productive, what didn't work well, and what additional actions you would take next time. (See appendix J for a sample format; you can also use this format for an in-progress assessment.)

42. Keep your resume (curriculum vitae) up to date.

A curriculum vitae is a resume for someone who isn't looking for a job just now. Moreover, it takes time to develop a well-written, polished resume. Having one on hand enables you to share your background easily with people interested in you and enables you to be considered for positions on short notice without having to start from scratch. It also helps build your reputation in the fields in which you work by helping to document your accomplishments. In essence, it can serve as a repository of your job-related accomplishments, career interests, special skills, and the unique and wonderful person that is . . . you've got it! You!

* * *

For review purposes, Figure 5-6 below contains a summary of each action you can and must take to launch a career in the nonprofit sector.

**Figure 5-6: Summary of the forty-two steps to a
nonprofit organization job**

Strategies for Research

1. Start with who you really are.
2. Have your goal(s) clearly in mind.
3. Complete the Job Change Worksheet of Appendix E (if you are now working).
4. Get a good "workplace" from which to conduct your search.
5. Start your search from your own strengths and contacts.
6. Use your placement office.
7. Make it easy for people to help you.
8. Do careful research on the sector and organizations in which you're interested (see appendix G).

Strategies to Get Your Foot in the Door

9. Use a variety of approaches for each potential position.
10. Do some volunteer work.
11. Develop a mentor.
12. Develop one or two good resumes.
13. Conduct your search in a well-organized fashion and be systematic (see figure 5-1).
14. Review professional journals and the major newspapers carefully and religiously (in acceptable geographic locations).
15. Construct a job search resource binder (see appendix H).
16. Consider involvement in a local or regional political campaign.
17. Take a course in nonprofit organization management.
18. Use a calendar to plan each week of your search (see figures 5-2, 5-3).
19. Do something everyday.

20. Give priority to those actions with greatest potential for getting you a job.

Strategies for the Interview

21. Make the interview work for you.
22. Be prepared for every interview (see figure 5-4).
23. See someone with potential hiring power whenever possible.
24. Do several practice interviews.
25. Don't take affronts personally.
26. Get prepared to deal with rejection.
27. Reach out for help if you need it.
28. Be tireless.
29. Treat this process as a full-time job.
30. Be almost ruthless.
31. Be positive.
32. Let search firms know of your availability if you are seeking a senior position.
33. Treat every interviewer as a client.
34. Be prepared for the tough question.
35. Be flexible and schedule more time than you think you'll need for the interview.

Strategies to Improve Your Chances

36. Thank all your contacts.
37. Be prepared to "close that sale" on the job you want.
38. Be accessible by phone.
39. Assess offers carefully and systematically (see figure 5-5, appendix L).
40. Help others once you are working.
41. Critique your job search performance once hired.
42. Keep your resume up to date.

NOTES
Chapter 5

1. Richard Bolles quoted in Joyce Cohen, "Helpful Hints for a Happy Job Change," *New York Times*, 14 October 1984, Section 12, p. 49.

2. Peter Grancretter, as cited in Marcia R. Fox, *Put Your Degree to Work* (New York: W.W. Norton & Co., 1979), 58.

3. William H. Morin and James C. Cabrera, *Parting Company, How to Survive the Loss of a Job and Find Another Successfully* (New York: Harcourt Brace Jovanovich, 1982), 247ff.

4. The Foundation Center is located at 79 Fifth Avenue, 8th Floor, New York, N.Y. 10003.

5. Daniel J. Levinson, *The Seasons of a Man's Life* (New York: Ballantine Books, 1978), 97ff.

6. For further guidance on question preparation, see, for example, Robert G. Traxel, *Manager's Guide to Successful Job Hunting*, New York: McGraw-Hill, 1978.

7. Ibid, 11-12.

WHAT IF? APPROACHING NPOs FROM WHERE YOU ARE

Job seekers contemplating a career in the nonprofit sector have a number of common questions and concerns. The best news is that others have successfully faced these questions and found answers that made it possible for them to pursue happy, productive lives in this sector. The same may turn out to be true for you. This chapter provides additional advice, specific to particular backgrounds, to be used in your nonprofit job search in conjunction with the steps presented elsewhere in this book.

What if I'm still a college student?

Horray for you, Mr./Ms. Student! You are already beginning to distinguish yourself by thinking about the important subject of a career before it is upon you (or, as can be the case, not available to you). Now let's turn to some specific suggestions.

1. *Start relating your curriculum to career planning early.*
    a. If you are an undergraduate, don't be unsettled if you find yourself changing your mind once or twice. But start to think about and explore alternatives early. Use your summer jobs to learn about future work options. Volunteer to work at occupations you might like to develop.
    b. If you are a graduate student, be more aggressive and precise about making explicit the relationship between what you study and what you hope to do.
    c. Use your college or graduate school advisers, but try to get the one or two who are known to be the most knowledgeable, caring, and sensitive to the concerns of students. And, if any know the nonprofit sector well, ask them in particular to help.

d. Use your school or university career counselor, who is often a different person from your academic advisor, with different skills and contacts. These people can help you understand the state of the job market. You may also need to reach out to senior executives in your field of interest, since not all career counselors will be particularly familiar with the nonprofit sector.

e. Investigate both the areas of academic skills (those acquired in an academic setting) and experience (those acquired by doing, e.g., internships, graduate assistantships, and the like).

f. Follow success. Find out which organizations most like the ones for which you might like to work have already hired graduates of your school. Talk with them. It wasn't that long ago that they faced your very problems. Use contacts with school clubs and academic and professional societies to learn more about people who do things that involve your interests.

2. *Consider obtaining a master's degree in nonprofit sector management at one of the colleges or universities now offering them.* A master's degree may not be for everyone, especially one focused upon the nonprofit sector. But the quality and variety of the course offerings in such programs is beginning to improve, making some of these programs worth exploring (see appendix C). Even if you are not interested in a course of study leading to a degree, you may want to take one or two individual courses. You will both learn something and make some contacts.

However, in selecting courses or a program you may find it helpful to ask these kinds of questions:

- What process was used to develop this curriculum?
- What is the background and experience of the majority of the instructors? More specifically, do the instructors have any direct nonprofit sector operating experience?
- What are the backgrounds of the students likely to take the course or program?
- Does the college or university have any information on the postgraduation employment experience of this program's graduates? Might I contact one or two of them to enrich my understanding of the value of this program?

3. *Take some economics, finance, budgeting, and accounting.* Many inhabitants of the nonprofit sector entered and grew through

the service delivery "side of the house." As a result, skills in these subjects have been neither widely held nor highly valued in the nonprofit sector until recently. As resource scarcity comes to the fore (again) there will be a growing premium on these skills.

4. *Beef up your analytical skills.* If you are afraid of numbers, find a course, a teaching assistant, a tutor, or a significant other who can help you overcome this fear. I used to teach a segment of one at the New School for Social Research called "Fingers & Toes: Quantitative Policy Analysis Made Easy." Many Graduate Schools of Public Administration, Government, Political Science, Public Health and Urban Planning have courses on Policy Analysis or Budget Analysis. Try it . . . you'll like it!

5. *Do get good grades.* Prospective employers note whether you have bothered to distinguish yourself academically, but you should also work on developing other aspects of yourself (i.e., people and social skills). However, although grades are considered, they become less important over time. And many other factors such as your performance and experience, overall type and level of education, how you fit into the work unit and the organization's culture (to the extent it is understood) all matter as much, if not more.

6. *Practice communicating quickly and well in writing.* Learn to take care with papers you write. There is a shortage in the work force of competent writers. Find opportunities to practice. Take them! Write often, regularly and with discipline.

7. *Polish your speaking ability!* Practice, practice, practice. Run for student office. Campaign for a friend or someone you admire. Join a debate team. Do anything; just practice!

8. *Learn to type!* It will improve your computer keyboard literacy and enable you to word process, as well as manipulate data more quickly.

9. *Prepare a complete draft of your resume and then revise it as you go.*

10. *Look for opportunities to work more intimately in projects that involve activities similar to what you think you would like to do.* Experiential education, learning by doing, is a superb way to acquire and polish most skills. Outward Bound, one of my favorite nonprofit organizations, uses this approach in its wilderness classrooms.

11. *Read more about the sector and working in it.* Need I say more?

12. *Don't be overly concerned if you are not sure about what you want to do.* Some of us still aren't sure what we want to do when we

grow up, even after several decades in the labor force. The best way to find out is to get out there and try one of the jobs.

13. *Remember that the learning process is uneven and can often be characterized by a pastiche of surprise, serendipity, and sweat!* As John W. Gardner, the founder of Common Cause and former Secretary of Health, Education and Welfare, said recently, "We love to tell young people the orderly way in which we decided we had to learn something and learned it. But the really great learning experiences are anything but orderly. We are like a very small child caught up in a very big wave."[1]

14. *Work part time.* It brings in money and provides experience, training, and a little humility.

What if this is my first job search?

We all have to do each thing in life for the first time once. Everyone you know who is now working did it for the first time once. That doesn't make it less scary at first, but you will survive it quite readily. Honest!

There is little specialized advice for you beyond this assurance, but I hope it feels right to you. You will survive, quite handily. Think about the search for your first position as a real adventure. Explore a new territory. Test alternatives that might be more difficult once you begin on a career path. Take risks. Try new things. Try something you have always wanted to do. Don't be afraid to fail.

Don't be afraid to reach high. Continue to explore widely. You only get to look for your first job one time. Make it the best adventure you can! Have some fun!

What if I'm thinking about a job change <u>into</u> the sector?

You won't find a simple answer here. Start by looking yourself in the eye in the mirror. What does that reflection say when asked, "Is it time to make a change?" If you (or the reflection) aren't sure, read over the Job Change Worksheet in appendix E.

There are also some danger signals which, if you are experiencing several of them at once, might be a hint that you should weigh the pros and cons regarding a change seriously. Here are a few of them:

- You hate to get out of bed most mornings, especially on work days.
- You dread going into work.
- You get little satisfaction from work. It's "just a job."

- You feel your work is seldom recognized or rewarded.
- You don't like your boss or many of your co-workers.
- You feel out of step all of the time with the organization and many of the people who work there.
- You don't feel as if you have learned much lately, and your skills are withering.[2]

This type of careful self-assessment approach is very healthy. You should look hard at the advantages your current position provides and how your position and the organization have contributed to your current progress.

If you are contemplating a career change, there are also a number of issues such as pay, location, benefits, working conditions, work values, and managerial style that you need to consider. Moreover, you are not alone. Lots of nonprofit sector people have had careers in government or business. In most instances, their prior experience turned out to be very useful.

What if I'm thinking about a job change <u>within</u> the sector?

Most of the ground rules and processes are the same but there are some additional considerations.

- Are you sure you have done the best you can with your current situation? Perhaps there are some actions you might take to enhance your current work or restructure your job.
- If it is time to move on, evaluate carefully and thoroughly those factors you do and do not like about your current position. Be very candid with yourself about your own strengths and weaknesses so you can work to find the best "fit."
- Use your network of friends and colleagues. Depending on your job situation, you may need to be cautious here. Confidentiality may be crucial to sustaining your current position. You may even find that, after some preliminary search work, your current position looks pretty good.
- Don't rush a search. If you become serious about making a change, look carefully. Take your time. Don't take the first opportunity to get out of a bad situation.
- Remember you have talent! Hang in there!

What if my only experience is in the private or public sectors?

How fortunate you are in approaching the nonprofit sector from either of the two other major sectors in our economy! Both of them have the substance and aura of providing extremely useful experience for the nonprofit sector.

The private sector, for example, is thought by many to be the place where well-managed and aggressive organizations reside. You can bring to nonprofit-sector work a host of contacts and skills you have developed in the private sector. You will need to pick up the NPO jargon. But, this is a do-able task. (See appendix K.) You also may need to raise your consciousness about the real social issues underlying that jargon, though this task may already be on your agenda.

If the public sector has been your domain in recent years, you have much to offer to the nonprofit sector. Much of the financial fuel driving the nonprofit sector's engines comes from the public sector. And, nonprofit organizations are heavily influenced by public policy decisions. You are coming right out of that territory! More important, the vast majority of issues addressed by NPOs are also explored in the public sector.

Finally, public sector people generally have a particular sensitivity to the need for and the tactics of dealing with diverse constituencies. Nonprofit sector organizations also have a variety of constituencies to which they must relate effectively if they are to be successful. Your experience and sensitivity to these matters can enhance substantially the contributions you can make to a nonprofit organization.

Rejoice in the fact that you have picked up a lot of valuable experience in that forty miles of good and bad road we call life. A great deal of this experience is valuable and transferable to the nonprofit sector. Maybe not all directly or not all immediately, but, you have been there!

John Gardner, the founder of Common Cause, offered several choice observations on these topics in a speech to foundation representatives:

> We learn from our jobs. We learn from our friends and families. We learn by accepting the commitments of life by playing the roles that life hands us, by getting older, by suffering, by taking risks, by loving, and by bearing life's indignities with dignity.
>
> The things we learn in maturity are not simple things such as acquiring information and skills. That is for youngsters. (I define youngsters as people under fifty.) We learn not to burn up energy in anxiety. We learn to manage tensions if we have any, which we do. *We learn that self-pity and resentment are among the most toxic of drugs.* (Emphasis added.)
>
> Those are things that are hard to learn early in life. As a rule we have to have picked up some mileage and some dents in our

fenders before we understand. As Norman Douglas said, 'There are some things we cannot learn from others, we have to pass through the fire.' And we can keep our zest until the day we die. If I may offer a simple maxim, be interested. Everybody wants to be interesting—but the vitalizing thing is to be interested. Keep a sense of wonder and curiosity. Discover new things. Risk failure. Reach out. Care.

If we are optimistic, it had better be a tough-minded optimism. We have to believe in ourselves, but we must not imagine that the path will be easy. It is tough as hell. Life is painful, and rain falls on the just, and Mr. Churchill was not being a pessimist when he said, 'I have nothing to offer but blood, toil, tears and sweat.' He had a great deal more to offer, but as a good leader, he was saying it was not going to be easy. He was also saying something that all great leaders say constantly—that failure is simply a reason to strengthen resolve.[3]

What if I'm now unemployed (because I was fired, RIF'd, sick for a long time, or laid off)?

First, let's start with the facts:

- It did happen.
- Whether it was fair or unjust, it still did happen.
- You are not alone. It has happened to many others who found new, rewarding jobs.
- It still hurts. You bet it does!
- There are many things you can do, if you pull your socks up and get started—that is what this book is all about!

Second, get on with the job search. Follow the basics outlined earlier in this book, especially the part about doing something every day. But you may also be concerned about how to explain to others what happened to you (i.e., being fired, RIF'd, etc.). There isn't any magic potion to make this situation disappear. But you don't need to even try. Instead, try some of these actions:

- If you were terminated by someone and you need his or her positive help now, call and reintroduce yourself. Explain that even though things did not work out well there you have grown, learned a lot, changed your attitude, or whatever is appropriate for you. Ask the person to emphasize the positive in any reference checks (without suggesting he or she say things that are untrue), and give you an opportunity to get "back on course."

- If the reason for leaving a job is asked in application materials, you can put in a notation that you will discuss this matter in the interview.
- If you need to explain what happened, there are some options outlined by Wright in his book on *Hardball Job Hunting Tactics:*

   a. "I had a personality conflict with my supervisor— I don't why, it just happened . . . .It was probably both of our faults.
   b. "I felt the job had been misrepresented and I did not know how to deal with it at the time, so I reacted badly, but I have grown as a result.
   c. "At the time I had personal problems that kept me from performing to the best of my ability. These have been solved and I am now able to make a positive contribution to a company."[4]

There are also some very specific, concrete actions you can take to help you turn this situation around. Here are a few:

1. *File for unemployment compensation immediately.* Your employers have paid unemployment taxes for years on your behalf. You are now in the exact situation for which this program was designed. Don't bother indulging in any false pride. Get your application forms filed now! It will also boost your morale to see some cash coming in!

2. *Start your job search activities immediately.* (Right after you file for unemployment compensation.) It will be tempting to clean the attic, repaint the house, visit Aunt Minnie, or take a vacation. Skip all of the above. Get to work finding work!

3. *Hunker down!* You already know it is going to be tough out there at times. You can prepare yourself for a bit of rejection. Ask your family and friends to circle the wagons just a little tighter. Nearly everyone is a bit scared, and *nearly everyone* gets down in the dumps once in a while during the job search process: Just don't let a short-term case of the blues stop you from acting *every day!*

   - *Invest in your job search.* Tighten up your personal and family budget but spend money to follow good leads. Dress as if you were doing very well . . . and you will be soon. (Although for many NPOs fancy work clothes aren't important.) Be sensitive to the mores of each NPO. Take

cues from other people who work there, the location, layout, and decoration of the office.
- *Don't falter, ever.* Keep moving, even when you hurt. Especially if you hurt. By keeping on the go you will keep your job search "muscles" warm and loose and your morale much higher. You will also secure a better job sooner.

What if I'm a woman returning to the labor force (after having a baby, being a housewife, or obtaining a degree)?

For whatever reasons, you haven't been in the regular work-for-pay work force for a while. That is not the end of the world, so don't waste time or energy worrying about things you can't change. The key people in most nonprofit organizations not only understand these things, they can be fairly sympathetic, especially if you help them to reach the right conclusions about you and the many good things you have to offer their NPO. The key goal is for you to articulate some very concrete ways in which you can be particularly helpful to your prospective employers now.

First, don't be afraid of trying the volunteer route. Many of the people you met in chapter 4 started as volunteers. And, they made the transition quite well! Joan Welsh, after raising a family, first volunteered in the battered women's movement, helped start a shelter in her community, and ended up as executive director of the shelter. She also served as a volunteer Chair of the National Coalition Against Domestic Violence. In fact, she recently started a new career as the Director of California Program Development for the Pacific Crest Outward Bound School.

Lois Roisman was Volunteer of the Year in Oklahoma City, started as an administrative assistant in the local community foundation and ended up a few years later as the executive director of the Jewish Fund for Justice. There are countless other stories, each affirming that excellent contacts are built and exposure created by executing well a good volunteer position.

Second, be of good cheer. Although it is difficult to document with more than anecdotal evidence, women seem to have more ready access to jobs and promotion opportunities in this sector. Yes, many are entry-level, but good people can move to the top—we are hungry for talented, hard-working people in this sector.

Third, start using the new "old-girl" network. Although the "old-boy" network never worked as well as many women believe (especially if you didn't go to an automatic-network eastern school), there is a growing network of successful women who are willing to help others. Threaded through some portions of this network are a number of men who are firmly committed to recruiting the best possible talent into the nonprofit sector. The best way to tap into this network is to get out there and interview and make contacts. The network is informal—many of its members never even think of themselves as "members."

Fourth, browse through the burgeoning literature at your local library or bookstore. There are many books to help women with the world of work. For those interested in the nonprofit sector, some of those that treat how to assess and explain to others the skills you have developed as a homemaker and volunteer may prove especially useful.[5]

Fifth, contact some of the special resources just for women in your area. However, caveat emptor! Check with other women who have consulted with these groups. If the information isn't helpful, move on quickly![6] Catalyst, an organization that offers many programs for women returning to the workplace, is one such resource that is located in New York City. See appendix G for additional resources.

Sixth, don't be afraid to explore flexible hours or job-sharing. There are lots of different ways to skin the career "cat"—you won't get the sale unless you ask.

Seventh, be positive. Don't assume doors will be closed to you. Go after what you want. Assume reasonable positions are attainable to you. Recognize that this sector is generally more open to women. Assume this to be the case.

The folks at New Ways to Work or APTP can help you as job seeker or employer look clearly at job sharing and part-time options; be sure to write them for more information if this is the avenue you seek.

What if I want to share a job and work part time?

Job sharing is one major route to working less than full time. It is growing in popularity. There are a number of very useful and practical ways to share a job which are explained in a delightful and informative book by Barney Olhmstead and Suzanne Smith, *The Job Sharing Handbook,* published by Ten Speed Press, Berkeley, California. In the early 1970's they formed an organization called New Ways to Work which is based in San Francisco (149 Ninth Street, San Francisco, CA 94103).

Another excellent resource on the topic is the Association of Part-Time Professionals, 7655 Old Springhouse Road, McLean, VA 22102. Since its founding in 1978, APTP has been an active advocate of part-time job opportunities throughout society at the professional level. Today, this national association has a job bank and several reportedly excellent publications, among them *Employee Benefits for Part-Timers*, *Part-Time Professional* (how to get, convert, or create a part-time job), and *Part-Time Work: A Bibliography.*

Job sharing can help reduce "new hire" costs and on the job training. It can also provide opportunities to do phased retirements, implement affirmative action programs and soften the unemployment consequences of work force reductions. For employees who wish to secure part-time employment, job sharing can be an excellent opportunity to work in more responsible positions with an interesting partner.

What if I belong to an ethnic, religious, racial, or other minority group?

The most constructive action you can take about historical inequity is to secure a rewarding position and change any such behavior within your spheres of influence. This is easier said than done, but it generally seems to be easier done in the nonprofit section than in other sectors.

As to getting the position, most of the basic ground rules in this book apply to you as well. And, yes, it may be more difficult. Although the nonprofit sector is not without prejudice, there is a more open and receptive attitude in the main. And, progress seems to keep taking place, albeit slowly.

If you feel the need for some specialized resources, Bolles' *Parachute* contains useful appendices on books for women, minorities, handicapped job hunters, and ex-offenders. Wright's *Hardball Job Hunting Tactics* also contains useful material for ex-offenders.

What if I'm an older teenager (or parent of one) thinking about work and life?

As Anita Manning, in a June 23, 1983 piece in *USA Today* said, "Many of us grew up like pinballs, bouncing willy-nilly from one major life event to another, without ever having stopped to find out who we are." It is hard, but so exciting to be growing up in our country today. The information and technology explosion has made

119

the securing of a complete education much more difficult—there is just much more to learn.

And, there are so many pressures. Young people grow up so quickly. And, they are so much more mature and, in most cases, responsible. I have learned a great deal in recent years from my fifteen-year-old daughter, Wyeth. Despite the challenges of raising two parents on different coasts, Wyeth is a mature, sensitive young woman who is fortunate to attend a caring yet rigorous Quaker high school in New York City, Friends Seminary. I have learned from Wyeth (not as well as I might, I concede) that young people can handle far more responsibility than we might originally be willing to allow; are more caring than those of us from the 1960's give them credit; face problems and pressures we barely understand; and will serve their country, their world and themselves very well indeed if we would just empower them enough to get on with their job!

If you are struggling to raise your parents (or help them raise you) there are some useful tools available to you. A wonderful set of three books has recently been produced by Advocacy Press, P.O. Box 236, Santa Barbara, California 93012. These are *Choices: A Teen Woman's Journal for Self-Awareness and Personal Planning; Challenges: A Young Man's Journal for Self-Awareness and Personal Planning;* and *Workbook for Choices and Challenges,* all by Mindy Bingham, Judy Edmondson, and Sandra Stryker. Moreover, if you are a teacher, a parent, on the curriculum committee or the school board, you will be pleased to know that, as a *Los Angeles Times* staff writer recently put it: "At Laguna Beach High School, where life as a high school junior or senior is generally carefree, a 'life-planning' course teaches a fourth R: Reality." The courses using these wonderful materials focus on some very practical aspects of learning. The classes generally provide a caring and nurturing environment. The students seem to get thoroughly involved, and they help students become more aware of options and possibilities in their lives.

As a teen, you can order and use these materials yourself. You might even grab the ball and help get a course installed in your own high school. As a parent, you could make these materials available to your daughter or son . . . and their friends. And, as Jim Sanderson of the *Los Angeles Times* put it in his November 3, 1983 "Liberated Male Column": "Every feminist who feels sick at heart that the Equal Rights Amendment failed can also do it. This is one candle you can light instead of cursing the darkness of sexual injustice. The teen daughter may not be your own, but you can buy this book and ask her mother (and her father) if you can spend some time with this young creature, exploring her dreams and helping her to become a confident survivor in today's tough world."

The materials help you as a young woman, for example, to complete a series of mind-stretching exercises that are also fun! You can:

- Envision your life in ten-year increments: where you will live, your jobs or major activities and the people closest to you.
- Develop a better understanding about how attitudes (yours and those of others) can limit your opportunities or help you succeed.
- Grasp vividly the meaning of different occupations in terms of the:
  - skills required to succeed at them
  - education usually needed to enter them
  - financial rewards that come from that line of work. They quote Paula Nelson, an economist: "The making of money is not a sex-linked skill. Women can and are turning it all around. We are discovering for ourselves the challenge—and the joy—of money."

The materials also help you, without lecturing, to discover for yourself facts about living many adults don't learn until too late. They help young people learn about budgeting for:

- The cost of financing a home, including down payments, interest, homeowners insurance, operating and maintenance charges
- Transportation
- Clothing
- Children
- Food
- Entertainment
- Furnishings
- Health care
- Child care
- Saving and other miscellaneous items

You can also explore some of the things you believe about life (values) and begin to clarify the different roles work might play in your life. You also can use these materials to set very concrete, attainable goals—something useful in life for all of us. And finally, you can learn some very useful things about making decisions through all of the major steps: (1) stating the decision to be made clearly, (2) identifying the major alternatives, (3) gathering information about the alternatives in order to evaluate them, and (4) considering the likely outcomes. *Choices'* authors provide some very helpful material on decision making patterns that we all use. They also provide you with lots of other practical advice on early career planning, family planning, securing financial aid to go on to college, working earlier and a host of other aspects of life that may be important to you.

Good luck!

What if I'm a retired or retiring business executive?

Many retired or retiring business executives, and line workers for that matter, have happily located positions in the nonprofit sector. Many of the most satisfied are the ones who have been able to secure responsible or at least influential positions as a volunteer.

For example, the National Executive Service Corps helps match retired executives with NPOs in need of their particular skills as consultants. Direct service provision, perhaps a bit different from your most recent line of work, may be more to your liking.

Just begin your search by contacting nearby NPOs. Write down your key interests and a few statements about what you would like to offer to an NPO. Be clear if you are going to volunteer or if you are seeking partial or full pay. Don't forget that a volunteer position can sometimes lead to a paying position later . . . and, that many NPOs have to keep volunteers as volunteers because they can't afford to pay!

There are also opportunities to do part-time work as a volunteer. You can exchange flexible hours at important and meaningful work with a nonprofit organization in return for no wages save the pleasure of providing help that is probably needed very badly.

If you discover the work is meaningless, move on. There are a number of NPOs that do need extra help with tasks important to the organization.

What if I wish to leave the clergy or religious life?

You are considering an important and most difficult decision. But, you have several things going for you! Those personal convictions about the worth of your fellow humans and the spiritual roles you have played in the service of humankind will now serve you well in a new career of service in the nonprofit sector. In the paragraphs below we will discuss some cautions and some special concrete, specific suggestions just for you.

On the cautionary side, please consider that:

- The nonprofit sector (as does the rest of "non-religious" life) contains most of the human and institutional irritants which may be distressing you now about religious life. That's right, the grass may not be much greener when you get to the other side of the fence, but it will be of a different variety.
- Not everyone in the nonprofit sector has the same degree of fervor or commitment to their work (which is not to be naive that all persons religious contain equal levels of same). For some, work in the nonprofit sector is a calling, but for others, it is just a job—nothing more.
- You aren't about to become wealthy. Depending on how you have been compensated in the past, your lifestyle may or may not be about to improve.
- Examine carefully if you really wish to continue in "human service" work. It may be that, given the reasons you are considering leaving religious life, you are ready for a complete break and respite from this genre of human problems. You may find you would be both happier and more productive in business. Don't reject this possibility without some careful thought.

On the more hopeful side, there is plenty of good news and some concrete suggestions.

- Your life and work experience are highly transferable to this sector. A number of the positions which you have held are quite likely to be replicated rather precisely in this sector. Do a few informational interviews to identify more specifically the kinds of positions you have already filled within your religious organization, and be sure to emphasize them in your resume.
- Emphasize the personal counseling/human sensitivity experiences and skills that many religious persons regularly must use. Weave this special skill and experience into the descriptions of your past work.
- Use vigorously and without hesitation the substantial network of those who have travelled the road before you. They are out there. Find them. Ask for help. Don't be bashful or ashamed. You must use these potentially powerful and useful contacts. You can repay this help by helping constructively those who choose to follow you. Remember the help you receive now, and

you will be able to repay it ten-fold with sensitivity and kindness.

- Investigate whether your religious organization itself or former religious persons may have established either an outplacement office or function within your religious organization . . . or whether a nonprofit organization might exist which pays particular attention to the special new career needs of former persons religious. For example, there is an organization called TRANSITION, 2000 Aldrich Avenue South, Minneapolis, Minnesota 55405, (612) 874-0104. TRANSITION is a warm, friendly nonprofit organization that serves church professionals in career change. Their fees are $600 for all services, including one in-take session, two follow-up sessions, the services of a professional psychologist (limit of three sessions), job seeking training, career assessment and counseling, a number of group support sessions, and testing. There is also a women's support/therapy group available to help women deal with both personal issues and the changing lifestyle matters attendant with career change out of religious circles. They provide a scholarship for $500 of the $600 fee, and are flexible about when and how they collect the remaining $100. What a terrific program!

Another example is a program called OPTIONS, jointly sponsored by:

- The American Lutheran Church
  Office of Support to Ministries
  422 South Fifth Street
  Minneapolis, Minnesota 55415
  (612) 330-3241

- The Association of Evangelical Lutheran Churches
  12015 Manchester Road, Suite 80LL
  St. Louis, Missouri 63131
  (314) 821-3889

- The Lutheran Church in America
  Division for Professional Leadership
  Department of Leadership Support
  2900 Queen Lane
  Philadelphia, Pennsylvania 19129
  (215) 849-5800

It is a *confidential* program with no reports issued to your bishops, congregations or anyone else. Their materials describe the program as practical, skill-oriented, confidential and personally-affirming: all attributes right on target! This program takes place six times per year, Monday noon through Sunday noon, at a retreat center at St. Mary's College, Leavenworth, Kansas 66048 (approximately 45 minutes from the Kansas City Airport, telephone (913) 682-5151. Participation is arranged through synod/district bishops. Spouses are encouraged to attend. Fee arrangements vary by church body but they are in the $150-$250 range for individuals/couples with the balance subsidized by the church body.

- Try to rekindle or touch closely those aspects which once gave you optimism about the future of humankind and the special calling which you have had. This work has prepared you well for working with others, even though you are now choosing to work with people in a different environment. Moreover, give some hard, honest thought to whether you might enjoy less one-on-one contact with people and prefer, instead, working more with numbers, objects or processes. This analysis will give you some useful clues about the nature of the work you might pursue. And all of this work can, but not necessarily must, be in the nonprofit sector.

It might be useful to remind ourselves of the definitions used by the two helping organizations cited above to define the essence of what they stand for, and of the process in which you are now engaged:

- Option—"an act of choosing . . . the power or right to choose . . . freedom of choice" (OPTION).
- Transition—"n. a movement, development, or evolution from one form, stage or style to another; change" (TRANSITION).

What if I have secured an NPO volunteer position but now want (or need) to be paid for the work?

There is no easy route but my interviews across the sector assure me that it can often happen. Perhaps the Zen-like notion of receiving most when one seeks the least applies to this situation. You should not seek out volunteer positions *solely* because you want one of them to turn into a paying job. On the other hand, many people end up

125

entering the sector because one of their volunteer positions leads to a paying one. See Chapter 4 for some concrete examples.

The actions you can take to facilitate this event are:
- Do a first-rate job at your volunteer work.
- Keep your eyes and ears open for paid positions becoming available through turnover or expansion via a new government contract or foundation grant.
- Learn all you can about the organization, other organizations that provide the same services, and the entire segment in which the organization operates (e.g., the health care industry for a nonprofit nursing home).
- Attend relevant professional or "industry" meetings to get a sense of the types of work and problems within the sector.

Finally, be clear and honest with both yourself and your 'employer.' Don't expect others to know something if you don't tell them.

What if I haven't found an NPO job but have a good project?

You are in luck! Here is a classic opportunity to build your own job via good fund-raising efforts. There can be a very solid relationship between fund raising and job seeking.

Here is what you should do. Write down your idea in a solid project plan-format. Identify the most likely two or three NPOs in which the project should be housed. Identify several logical potential funding sources if you can. Suggest to the NPOs that you work with them to refine the plan, raise the money to carry it out, and then execute it once the money is in hand.

It won't be easy. Don't be afraid to approach several NPOs with the idea—but be up front with everyone if you are talking with several NPOs. And, while it may take a little longer, some of the most interesting jobs are the ones created by entrepreneurial job seekers! Good luck!

What if I'm asked to fill out an application form?

First of all, don't panic. Many organizations, including nonprofit organizations, use them. Second, take them seriously, for they may well be used as a simple screening device. Third, follow the instructions *to the letter.* If it says print, do so! Screeners of applications may use the fact that you either cannot or will not follow instructions to be an indicator that you won't follow instructions in the workplace either, or that you may have sloppy work or communication habits. Finally, get a few application forms from organizations and go over all the information you need to fill out the most comprehensive one. And be sure to carry that information with you whenever you are job hunting so that you can concentrate on legible writing and correct spelling when completing any application forms. See Chapter 5, Figure 5-4 and Appendix H.

If you are still extremely nervous about all or part of completing an application form, look at a book like Wright's *Hardball Job Hunting Tactics.*[7]

What if I still think I need help?

Most of this task of getting a new or first job does rest on your shoulders. But by now you've got a number of specific actions you can take to keep those shoulders from slumping on most days. But what if you feel you need help? There is lots of it available. But, caveat emptor! Let the buyer aware.

1. *Start with your friends*—for ideas, for referrals, for contacts, for moral support, for tender loving care.
2. *Touch base with your alma mater's career counseling and/or referral service.*
3. *Look for associations of both organizations and workers within the subsector of your interest,* such as, the Council on Foundations, the National Society of Fund Raising Executives, or the National Association of Social Workers.
4. *Talk to a few nearby organizations in which you might be interested for honest informational interviews.* (See Bolles' book, *What Color is Your Parachute?* for a discussion of the misuse of this kind of interview.)
5. *If you are totally confused about what you want to do, or work to which you might be best suited, consider exploring some of the various job search tests,* such as (a) interest inventories that help you identify the kinds of work you might enjoy doing (*if you have the skills for it*), and (b) "aptitude tests [that] reflect the kinds and degrees of innate capabilities you have."[8] The Strong-Campbell Interest Inventory and Meyers-Briggs Type Indicator are two such tests. You can get assistance with locating some of these tests and qualified test administrators through a good college counseling center or specialized programs in your area, such as the Career Counseling and Resources Center, School of Continuing Education, New York University, New York, New York.

6. *Finally there is additional help available in your local library, local college or university evening courses, local nonprofit organizations such as the YWCA in New York City,* which frequently offers career search and career counseling courses, and programs that specialize in courses and advice for women returning to the workplace, such as Catalyst in New York City.[9]

NOTES
Chapter 6

1. John Gardner, "Personal and Organizational Renewal" (Speech before the 36th Annual Meeting of the Conference of Southwest Foundations, Fort Worth, Texas, 5 April 1984).

2. Several of these danger signals were taken from or adapted from Traxel, *Manager's Guide*, 4.

3. Gardner, "Personal and Organizational Renewal."

4. Richard Wright, *Hardball Job Hunting Tactics* (New York: Facts on File Publications, 1983).

5. See Bolles, *What Color*, 286-88, for a listing of books and resources written especially for women.

6. Bolles, *What Color*, 324-333.

7. Wright, *Hardball*, 27 ff.

8. Gene R. Hawes, *The Encyclopedia of Second Careers* (New York: Facts on File Publications, 1984), 437.

9. For a more detailed discussion of evening courses, see Hawes, *Encyclopedia*, especially chapter 6.

PART III

AFTER THE OFFER

Chapter 7

ACCEPTING (OR REJECTING) THE JOB OFFER

Now you are where you were headed! Congratulations! You deserve it! Let the person making the offer know immediately how pleased you are to have been selected to receive an offer. After all, this is what this whole process is about, right?

If you feel any need to think it over, say so. In fact, in many situations I urge you to take a day or so to think it over. You can be most flattered by the offer, ask a few key questions, and then suggest that you sleep on it overnight or for one or two days. Few people will be overly distressed if you want one or two days to give their offer the careful consideration it deserves. You can indicate that you take this decision very seriously and want to weigh it carefully. Try to determine how urgently the prospective employer feels about getting a reply. Establish a clear, mutually agreeable and comfortable deadline by which you will communicate your answer. Be sure your contact will be in town for your communication or arrange another way to reach him or her.

IF YOU ARE LEANING TOWARD ACCEPTING THE OFFER . . .

You must be very pleased and excited. Just keep in mind that your bargaining leverage is now at its zenith. This is the best time, for those matters about which you are not already clear to:

- clarify
- specify
- negotiate
- bargain
- renegotiate.

I am not recommending you put a prospective employer through any wringers here; you just might end up convincing the employer to cancel the offer. However, any job offer has critical aspects that need to be assessed carefully. Some of the these are examined below. Don't wait until offer time to clarify all of the items. But, this section should serve as a helpful check list to nail down the details and make sure you have covered the key elements.

1. Negotiate a decent salary.

This is particularly important in the nonprofit sector because large salary raises generally seem more difficult in this sector to secure due to the limited resources available and the constant pressure to spend the maximum dollars on direct programs. Moreover, other means of enhancing one's salary such as stock options or bonuses are rarely available. One hopeful sign is that a few of the most adventurous NPO boards are beginning to explore some forms of incentive compensation tied to performance.

But how can you develop an intelligent negotiating posture? The best weapon you have is to do your homework and have gathered as much information in advance about the compensation practices of the segment of the sector in which you are going to be working and, more specifically, the organization making you an offer. Swell idea, you say, but how? Here are a few alternative actions you can take to help inform yourself before negotiating a salary:

- *Don't feel that you are being tacky or greedy to attempt to negotiate your salary.* There is nothing wrong with fully informing yourself and attempting to secure the best wage for yourself and others who may share in the shelter, food, and goods and services you purchase with your earnings.
- *Contact the local branch of the Department of Labor for data on comparative costs of living in various geographical areas.* This is particularly important to do if you are considering relocating. A 10 percent salary increase in a new location where the cost of living is 18 percent higher than your current place of residence may not be a very good deal from a strictly financial point of view.
- *Talk to people who now work for the NPO about compensation practices, at least in general terms.* It may have been a good idea to have explored this subject in a fairly low key way earlier in your interviews, especially when you have been brought into con-

132

tact with people your own age or near your organizational level. However, the time to concentrate on salary is after you have secured a job offer.

- *Do some concrete salary research.* You will find that there are a number of potential sources. You just need to polish your detective skills! For example, you may find useful information in the Form 990 filed by all organizations of any size with the IRS. But don't wait until the last minute to go after these unless you know that microfilms of them are available in a local research library. These 990s contain, most of the time, compensation information for the senior officers and executives of NPOs. By projecting, you can develop some sense of the likely compensation levels "down the line."

    You may also find that the local United Way or community planning agency has done a salary survey for your area of the country and the type of NPO for which you are considering working. The local budget bureau, office of management and budget, or county planning department may have some useful salary data, especially for comparable positions that exist in both NPOs and government units. In addition, you may find the local chamber of commerce or business association has data on the going rate for a number of positions common to both the nonprofit and private sector. Finally, you may get some useful data from organizations of professionals working in such NPOs (e.g., the local chapter of the National Association of Social Workers) or trade unions representing workers in your NPO (e.g., hospital workers' local).

- *Let the person making you the job offer make the first move on salary.* The NPO may have a higher figure than you did in mind and there is no reason to "show your hand" prematurely.

- *Don't assume that the initial offer is necessarily the final or firm one.* Some people as well as some organizations expect and even enjoy some negotiating. Be sensitive to the reactions you are getting through the process. Some organizations will have very fixed levels for each position with prescribed ranges. Talk candidly with your contact in order to understand how wages are set and administered. And be sensitive to the operating style of the people with whom you are dealing. A rough-and-tumble negotiation is just right for one person and greedy, aggressive, and obnoxious to another. Get to know the style and personality of interviewers early on and speak with them "in their language."

- *Consider salary as the primary, but not the only, element of your total compensation package.* Later in this chapter we will explore the other elements of a compensation package. You may find that tradeoffs can be made in one element for another. But also keep in mind that salary is probably going to be the only steady immediate cash component. You can't pay your rent or mortgage with retirement benefits or vacation policies. Prepare a worksheet on which you will list the salary offer as well as the other elements of your entire compensation offer for comparison purposes. See Appendix L.
- *Learn about compensation review procedures*—but do not pin major hopes on "making it up later," if you accept a much lower offer than you feel is appropriate salary now. Such thinking has several fallacies. First, you start piling up dollar "losses" on day one. You have to earn every lost dollar back on top of all other raises for as long as you "lost" them just to break even. Thus, it is important to start as high as you can. Second, your current compensation level often is used as a guide for positions elsewhere. This notion is often inappropriate but still widely practiced.
- *Expect salary negotiating to be difficult and/or a bit stressful.* Most of us are embarrassed to talk about money, especially if it is money to be paid for our skills and talents. As Melvin Thomas, the author of *Why Should I Hire You,* said, "If hiring is emotional, then salary negotiating is hysterical."[1] On the other hand, you will only have to negotiate for your starting salary once for each position. Swallow hard once, do your homework, smile, and go for it!
- *Never give your own current compensation information to a prospective employer without at least one face-to-face interview.* It is preferable to leave the discussion of compensation to the end when both parties have concluded that they want to form an employer/employee partnership.
- *Don't falsely inflate your current salary information.* First of all, it is totally inappropriate to lie about anything in the interviewing process. Second, the facts could easily come out and cost you the job. However, if you are very close to receiving a scheduled cost-of-living increase or a merit raise, you are wise to acquaint your prospective employer with this fact.
- *Even if you think you can negotiate hard for your salary, do some practicing in advance.* Also, if you have other offers at higher amounts, be prepared to share them. Here are two fairly ag-

gressive approaches to negotiating an offer upward suggested by Melvin Thomas:

"Look Mel, I'm not asking for any guarantees, and you're not offering any. We've arranged a good marriage, and I think we both realize it. The $4,000 standing in our way is vitally important to me and my family. Mostly, though, it would be your vote of confidence. We both know what happens when a person doesn't measure up to his boss's expectations, and you're obviously convinced I'll perform or you wouldn't have hired me. So please treat me as a member of the team and not as an outsider. Now I'd like to plan on starting on the fifteenth if you have no objection." Or, you might try:

"Look Mel, if you wanted a $1.98 job done you'd be talking to a $1.98 person. You're good for me and I'm good for you and we both know it. We're talking about $4,000, which the company (read NPO) can readily afford and which I can't. Now if you have no objections, I'd still like to plan on the fifteenth as a starting date."

As Mr. Thomas puts it, "your new company will never permit you to forget your starting salary. Chances are it will be used as a means of measurement for any future salary increases."[2] Also remember that while it is useful to talk about rigorous negotiating, the content and atmosphere of the job are more important. The primary goal is to be happy about your work situation.

2. Negotiate hard but carefully for the balance of your compensation package.

All too many boards of NPOs still hold to the anachronistic notion that a substantial portion of the NPO worker's compensation should be of psychic income. The only problem is that it is very difficult to retire or educate children on savings from a psychic income.

There are a vast number of other items that might be included in your compensation package. In many ways, some NPOs have been extremely creative in their compensation arrangements, whereas others have done very little for their people. One strong note of caution in using the list of options below: Do not think for a moment that most NPO workers have all or even many of the options listed. The sector runs the full range from well compensated in the fullest sense of the word to being very poorly compensated. The list provides a means of comparing *all* of the elements of a compensation package with your own current situation. Or, it can be used as a shopping list to negotiate some flexibility in your compensation package. Here are some of the possible items:

- Bonuses—although rarely used now, there is growing interest in tying cash bonuses to concrete performance measures.
- Expense allowances—some NPOs allow work travel or commuting allowances, meal or parking allowances, or certain other regular payments beyond reimbursement for out-of-pocket expenses. One note of caution here; some NPOs do not fully reimburse for out-of-pocket expenses incurred while on NPO business. Try to negotiate full reimbursement of *reasonable* expenses.
- Insurance—see what the organization has to offer in the way of group life, group hospital, accidental death and disability, major medical, and dental insurance.
- Annual physical examination—preventive health care is usually cheaper than ameliorative care.
- Pension plan—be sure to look at the vesting policy (i.e., how many years must pass before the pension is fully yours).
- Matching investment or savings plan—nice though not too many NPOs have this feature yet.
- Deferred compensation—used more for senior executives.
- Voluntary salary reduction plan—which is contributed on a before-tax basis into a tax-deferred annuity or other investment plan managed by a mutual fund or insurance company. Note that some versions of these plans are only available to NPOs. Also keep in mind that the money you put in will be taxed when you take it out, but presumably this will be after you retire when your tax rate will be much lower. Some NPOs have both employer and employee contributions—others simply have employee contributions. If you can handle the strain on your current cash flow this is a very powerful and useful benefit.
- Transportation allowances, including mileage, gas, car, parking, or commuting allowances.
- Vacation, sick leave, and compensatory time off.
- Paid memberships in professional associations, health/athletic clubs, dining clubs, or similar groups.
- Direct disability pay.
- Subsidized legal assistance, financial planning assistance, tax advice or accounting assistance.
- Discounts or free services to family members.

- Subsidized home mortgage or access to loan money.
- Other housing allowance.
- Credit unions for saving as well as borrowing.
- Short-term loans.
- Time off to do freelance consulting or teach as a means of enhancing your professional skills and income.
- Reimbursement or subsidy for inservice or further academic training.
- Severance pay—it's awkward to discuss this one—you are just starting work. Perhaps you should simply read the personnel manual as soon as you can.

Remember that although many of these items are becoming used more widely, almost no NPO workers have all or even a majority of them. Appendix L contains a worksheet that can help you analyze all aspects of your compensation.

3. Review the organization's structure.

Give particular attention to lines of authority, chains of command, and *especially* communication channels. It is much easier to straighten out wrinkles before you are on board than afterward.

4. Discuss the key people in the major positions with whom you will work.

Try to develop some sense of how they perceive the position you will be filling, what their expectations are for the person in that slot, and what the historical issues, if any, are between the various positions. Note that it is preferable to meet them in the course of your interviews, if at all possible.

5. Discuss the job description in some depth with your immediate supervisor.

You may save some embarrassment on this question by having already learned whether such descriptions are commonly used in the organization. Try to get a sense of the major problems you will face and what resources are available to address these problems.

Don't try to have any concrete answers just yet for the problems identified for you; your goal at this point is to develop a good map of the territory. There will be plenty of time ahead for problem solving.

If no job description exists, don't rush in to create one too early. Try to allow yourself as much flexibility as possible in the early months.

6. **Ask for a short briefing on the key problems and issues faced by the organization, the nonprofit segment in which your NPO resides, and the department or unit in which you will work.**

Try to develop a sense of the NPO's current posture. Explore any differences in view between the board and the staff on how the issues should be addressed. This question will show you are both inquisitive and a grounded forward planner.

7. **Try to get a sense of the NPO's interest in and commitment to personal development.**

Ask about the extent of inservice training for yourself and the people who may be reporting to you. Also explore the extent to which external training and academic programs are available and utilized by the organization. You may wish to negotiate a commitment to some level of ongoing personal development as part of your compensation package.

8. **Explore the frequency and depth of personnel reviews.**

If you are particularly uneasy about the organization's commitment to this activity, you could ask to see a copy of one of their personnel review tools or worksheets. However, this is a generally a weak area for many NPOs and you may not get a positive response. Moreover, this request may be viewed as an intrusion. You will just have to play it by ear. You will also want to find out whether compensation changes are linked directly to personnel performance reviews. Don't despair if the response isn't what you would like to hear. This area may turn out to be one of those to which you can make a substantial contribution.

9. **Consider doing a few very discreet reference checks before accepting the job.**

Talk to a few of the organizations that work with the NPO or to a few of its clients. You could examine the board of directors or any board of advisers for comments with people you or close colleagues might know. However, this is a particularly sensitive area, so *tread very carefully.* Perhaps the best time to do much of this homework is before you go for your first interview.

Finally, having looked at as many factors as appear reasonable and negotiated the best compensation package you can, PLUNGE!

I hope you are facing this task because you have several offers in hand and have chosen the most attractive one.

IF YOU ARE LEANING TOWARD REJECTING THE OFFER . . .

If your careful interviewing and research have led you to conclude that the current position isn't the right one for you, what should you do? Here are a few simple suggestions.

1. Express true pleasure that you have been extended an offer to join the XYZ nonprofit organization.
2. Think the offer over very carefully, weighing the pros and cons.
3. If you must say no, be clear, concise and thoughtful. Don't burn any bridges. In this mobile society of ours, you may well run into the same people again.
4. Don't provide a lot of detail to explain the thinking behind your decision. If you want a discussion about the pros and cons of taking the job, be clear and pursue that topic. But if you have made up your mind, communicate your decision kindly but without a lot of window dressing.
5. Thank each person involved in the recruiting and interviewing process for their time. Mention that having the opportunity to meet them has made your decision much more difficult. Write personal notes if it doesn't seem appropriate to talk with them in person.
6. Finally, don't stop creating opportunities for yourself through tasteful and appropriate exposure. For example, continue to do volunteer work, maintain contact with key people in the nonprofit sector segments in which you work and continue your own professional development.

Notes
Chapter 7

1. Melvin R. Thompson, *Why Should I Hire You?* (San Diego, Calif.: Venture Press, 1975), 137.

2. Ibid., 138.

PREPARE TO MEET FUTURE CHALLENGES— Twenty-Four Key Issues Facing The Nonprofit Sector (And Those Who Work In It)

There are many key issues facing the nonprofit sector now and in the years ahead. Some of the more critical issues are presented here, each in the context of their impact on the nonprofit job market and job seekers. These issues are likely to affect the nonprofit sector at different levels: at the sector level; segments within the sector (e.g., the health care segment) and at the individual person's level (e.g., affecting the individual's ability to deliver health care).

Understanding these issues will help you enjoy a solid perspective on the sector in which you seek work. You will be able to approach each organization better prepared and able to interview more effectively if you have a better informed long-term view of events in the sector. Moreover, you have an opportunity to key into one or more of these issues and the trends that create them as another way of generating a job or becoming uniquely qualified for one. The key issues include:

1. The sector's government funding is now decreasing after a period of considerable government financial support.

The government sector has grown very rapidly and outpaced the nonprofit sector in recent years. The government's entry into previously nonprofit sector-dominated and controlled areas via financing direct service delivery and aggressive regulation has drastically changed the balance of power existing previously. This growth and heavy reliance on government funding is challenging fundamentally the old notion of independence in this "independent" sector.

This advent of a significantly larger role for government has led to "a change in the direction to which citizens now look for the fulfillment of their needs—to government rather than to themselves."[1]

There is also the double bind here brought by President Reagan's New Federalism. Current federal policy is pushing NPOs and the private sector to expand and do more while at the same time reducing its financial support from the government.

If NPOs are to rebalance the scales to some degree, they must engage in the political process. NPOs must define more crisply all of their relevant constituencies and accept some involvement in the formation of political interest groups, alliances, and power blocks. It will be difficult, but necessary if they are to be effective, for NPOs to overcome an institutional shyness regarding the political process.

Understanding how money flows through the government and which "levers" are most effective will be particularly highly prized skills in the future.

2. Some role reversal is taking place between government and the nonprofit sector.

The government traditionally picked up or was asked to pick up the cost of expanding model or experimental programs for new or better ways to deliver human services. Now, the government (at all levels) is asking grantmakers in the nonprofit sector, nonprofit organizations, and private citizens to assume the costs of a number of activities traditionally thought of as the government's responsibility (e.g., food or shelter for the destitute and homeless, research in a number of fields, performance measurement in the environment, and so on).

In addition, government in a number of subsectors is turning to for-profit organizations for executing some of its purchase-of-service agreements and other means of contracting out services, thus placing organizations in the nonprofit sector under increased competitive pressure and restricting or reducing the number of jobs in the sector.

3. There is an explosion of so-called professionalization.

A number of jobs within the nonprofit sector are becoming increasingly "professionalized." However, it is helpful to keep in mind that a wag once described a professional as someone who charged more than average and couldn't type. The anonymous wag's description of some of the so-called professionals in the nonprofit sector may well be accurate. Everyone contributes in an important way to the functioning of a nonprofit organization, whether in a white coat in the laboratory or the emergency room, or at the console of a sophisticated computer crunching numbers or an equally important word processor.

Nonetheless, it is true that a number of positions in the field are becoming the subject of turf battles for which "profession," or sometimes which collective bargaining unit for a professional group, will "get the job." For example, there have been attempts by teachers' unions to control the provision of day care. Some have argued this is a matter of control over jobs; others have argued that licensed teachers can do a better job because they have been trained in greater depth for the work. The implication for you is that there may be other forces at work beyond pure and traditional supply and demand.

In other cases there has been an attempt to make the requirements for certain positions carry with them a growing number of formal academic credentials. Sometimes such a move can upgrade the quality of training for the person holding the job. But increased credential requirements can also have the effect of preventing more grass roots people or those with less formal training from having access to these positions.

Moreover, as the credentials for holding many positions are raised and tied to academic credentials, people seeking to move up will need to seek advanced degrees, obtain inservice training, or take other steps to acquire these credentials.

Of course, one of the crucial issues for nonprofit organization boards and managers who permit, and even facilitate, this upgrading of credentials is whether the academic credentials are in fact correlated with the skills required to carry out the job effectively.

Another implication, for you as a job hunter, of this increased professionalization/credentialing is that many employers use credentials as a screening tool. Thus the "appropriate credentials" may be necessary to have "openers in the game" of those to be considered for a position.

There are also increased costs for both NPO managers and job seekers related to the increase in credentials and so-called professionalization. Persons who have spent the money and time to acquire advanced degrees or other professional credentials have a natural desire to recoup the costs of the time and money invested in acquiring these credentials. Thus they press for higher salaries (and tuition reimbursement whenever possible). These costs are to some degree passed on either to the consumer of the services or to third-party payers, such as governments, individuals contributing to the organization, United Ways and foundations.

4. A growing concentration of power and volume in the larger dominant institutions characterizes the sector.

According to the analysis of Lester Salamon of the Urban Institute, 4 percent of the nonprofit organizations account for roughly 70 percent for the sector's expenditures.[2] I have not located solid longitudinal data with which to compare this information, but the data suggest some rather high levels of resource concentration.

Since virtually all segments of the sector are fairly labor intensive (and somewhat equally so), the bulk of the jobs are also concentrated in a fairly small percentage of the organizations. But be of good cheer, you are only looking for one job, and the sector contains a number of small, independent, and quite flexible organizations, each of which has some employment potential.

5. The financial base of many, though certainly not all, NPOs is eroding.

Some NPOs are addressing this problem by developing a more aggressive marketing orientation. However, as discussed elsewhere, selective provision of services can eliminate those most in need of them. On the cost side, there is a more aggressive posture being developed by many NPOs to control costs and reduce them. This can stifle compensation adjustments but create some interesting job opportunities. Finally, government is an important source of money for most NPOs, so check on the recent trends in and extent of government support.

6. The shift toward more conservative politics and governance has been a mixed blessing for NPOs.

Reductions in financial allocations to purely government-operated agencies in various human services fields has reopened opportunities for action by NPOs. However, the federal shift in emphasis toward military expenditures and away from support of domestic social programs has hurt a number of agencies in the nonprofit sector.

NPOs are caught in the social debate over the role of government, the private sector, and the nonprofit sector. As the debate, even struggle, for definition continues, it is critical to think clearly and be realistic about both how much responsibility a sector can take as well as the flow of resources with which to finance the assumption of those responsibilities.

Certain NPO fields have been much harder hit by federal and state reductions than others. It may be useful to look at the current financial support trends to see what impact, if any, they have had on the particular subsegment of the sector in which you are interested.

There will be a particular demand for people who can bridge the chasm between so-called liberals and conservatives and:

- Communicate clearly
- Forge alliances
- Facilitate compromises
- Break the logjams of inaction

7. Growing competition for both government and contributed money has had both good and bad results.

Resources for NPO uses have always been limited in our society. However, depending on the historical moment and the problems being addressed, our society has demonstrated differing levels of awareness of these limits. The current times seem to be ones in which there is a growing awareness of and sensitivity to the limits of the resources available for nonprofit organization work. As a result, there is growing competition for the two major sources of NPO financial resources, government money and contributed money (from individuals, corporations, and foundations). The competition has not been entirely negative. It has stimulated a number of NPOs to do some beneficial things. For example, NPOs as a group seem to be

- Doing a better job of documenting their good work,
- Communicating more frequently and more clearly with their various publics—especially those with the potential for financial support, and
- Trimming the "fat" from less efficient programs.

This competition for financial resources has also expanded significantly the number of jobs for fund raisers. These people focus their efforts on helping the NPO solicit the public, the government, corporations, and foundations for contributions to pay for the people and

145

materials needed to carry out their NPO's mission. Fund-raising events are being held more frequently. The use of direct mail fund raising has increased dramatically. That means more jobs performing these functions. Not only are the number of fund-raising jobs expanding relatively rapidly, the compensation for these positions seems to be increasing faster than most other positions in the sector.

The tensions generated by the growing disparity between our society's identified social needs and the nation's ability and political will to commit resources to meet these needs is also building a premium for communication skills in the nonprofit sector. There will always be special opportunities for those who can articulate both the social problem and a "solution" that people can understand and buy into.

Finally, as the limits of financial resurces have become more clear to the majority of those who work in the nonprofit sector or direct its institutions, there is a growing use of more sophisticated financing mechanisms. For example, loan subsidies and interest "writedowns" are being sought more frequently by NPO managers. And the use of the tax-exempt nature of the NPO is being constructively exploited through bonding, buy- and lease-back arrangements, and the transfer of depreciation writeoffs. Of course, tax reform efforts may have an impact on some of these approaches.

The implication of this trend and others related to it is that there is a growing need for employees with an interest in and/or capacity to understand and use sophisticated financing techniques. Quantitative analytical skills will become increasing valued and sought. Electronic data processing and management information skills are becoming increasingly vital to the sector.

There is also a need for people knowledgeable about tax law and creative in its application.

8. The focus on earned income has opened up new opportunities.

As discussed in point number seven above, there is growing interest in expanding sources of earned income for nonprofit organizations. In a June 1984 speech in San Francisco at a Nonprofit Management Association Conference, Dr. Lester Salamon reported that over 70 percent of NPOs derive money from earned income sources. He also indicated that most of the recent increases in funds raised by NPOs had come from earned income.[3] This growing interest opens up some good opportunities for people with money-making skills and experience from disciplines such as marketing or backgrounds such as small business management. There is likely to be a growing premium on "plain old business sense," including:

- a better understanding of the financial implications of how NPO services are priced to recipients and third-party payers,
- marketing skills applied to NPO relations with clients, funders, and other constituencies, and
- a sense of the importance of sound strategic planning, to name just a few.

In addition, organizations in the nonprofit sector have also begun to expand their use of service fees. While increasing earned income is often a good thing for nonprofit organizations, according to Lester Salamon's analyses its increased use by NPOs is also likely to begin to change the mix of those being served by the NPOs. It would appear that as this trend continues, a growing number of NPOs will move away from serving those who are most in need financially. I am troubled by this trend and simply want to alert you, as a job seeker, to the issue. For, if serving the poor is part of your motivation, you will need to probe the service-pricing practices and the client mix of your potential employer carefully. You also may find yourself in a position to provide some leadership to a part of our society in terms of helping constructively those most in need.

You should also recognize as a potential new employee that this increased focus on earned income does not mean that the financial and human resources are going to be "on board" to do the job. Be cautious in tackling large earned-income projects unless the planning seems very solid and you are clear about the adequacy of the resources and the business plan. You also may be able to see some increased financial stability in the NPOs you examine since increased attention on earned income can expand and help stabilize the NPO's financial base.

9. The growing recognition of scarce and limited resources is placing an increasing premium on people with cost-control and cost-containment skills.

When there isn't enough money to go around (a fact becoming increasingly apparent), NPO boards of directors and senior management will look more aggressively for ways to stretch the money they do have. Rising costs are particularly difficult for the nonprofit sector to handle since many of its segments and organizations have little capacity to pass cost increases along to their "customers." In fact, many of these customers are using NPO services precisely because they are poor or in some kind of need or stress situation.

On the other hand, this high-cost-pressure situation presents you, the job seeker, with a special opportunity. If you have a way of providing some special skills, talents, or experience in reducing or containing particularly high-cost categories such as energy for NPOs you may have identified another inside track to a challenging and rewarding job—perhaps one created just for you. Some of the promising cost-containment areas in NPOs include: energy management, energy conservation, paperwork management, telecommunications, automation, fringe benefits, insurance, and many more.

For example, you may be able to help launch or join one of the "next wave" projects in cost-control and cost-containment such as the Nonprofit Energy Conservation (NOPEC) a project initiated by the New York Community Trust aimed at helping form local Energy Conservation Funds to assist NPOs in identifying, financing, and implementing energy conservation measures in buildings they own or in which they have long-term leases. You might look for a project such as the Telecommunications Cooperative Network, launched by Robert Loeb in New York to help nonprofit organizations reduce their telephone, other communications, and data processing costs. Similar projects are needed to strengthen facility management, reduce insurance costs, expand existing group purchasing programs, strengthen cash management procedures, and the like.

In summary, the interaction of rapidly rising costs and diminished or more slowly growing resources is putting an ever-higher premium and increased economic incentives on more effective resource management. There will be terrific job opportunities for those with the ingenuity to use resources more effectively and spend money "smarter" while caring about and wanting to work with nonprofit organizations and their constituents.

10. Competition with the private for-profit sector is growing.

As a result of this competition, NPOs may emulate private sector organizations by becoming more competitive in their operating style, increasing the use of incentive compensation, looking at deliberate reductions in service quality as costs rise, and using more classical marketing practices. And, more NPOs are providing their own insurance and pension plans. They are beginning to compete with the private sector by aggregating customers and expanding vertically to gain control of supplies and services in order to ensure their quality, quantity, and price.

Some of this competition is economic in nature. NPOs claim that for-profit organizations "skim the cream" in providing services to the easiest-to-serve segments, leaving the most difficult-to-serve (and expensive) to NPOs. One example is the widely reported practice of a number of for-profit hospitals dumping uninsured patients onto public or nonprofit hospitals. For-profit organizations, on the other hand, point out that NPOs compete with unfair tax and subsidy advantages, an issue in which the courts will be engaged in the near future. In segments such as hospitals, health care, and management consulting, for example, there is a blurring of the lines between for-profit and nonprofit organizations. There is head-to-head competition between organizations in these areas, contributing to their vitality but making employment in them perhaps just a tiny bit less stable.

Note that this competition is a two-edged sword. Some nonprofit segments may decline or disappear because of vigorous private sector competition due to better management, stronger capitalization, skimming the most profitable/least-cost clients, more aggressive marketing, stronger financial incentives for employees, and a variety of other reasons. Other NPOs will be strengthened by a combination of the contest and their own ingenuity.

11. NPOs are increasingly entering the political arena and with growing sophistication and skill.

As Waldemar Nielsen stated, "The new era is one of socialization and politicization, of complexity and interconnection."[4] Since large (even if declining for some segments) amounts of money come from government sources, it seems likely that those NPOs with either the most direct political power or influence are likely to be able to influence the allocation of scarce public resources away from the programmatic approaches of organizations without political influence. This generalization will, of course, be honored often in the breach since many public managers and political persons are capable of dispensing large amounts of public money with no political input from potential recipients.

NPOs are also likely to band together in affinity groups to lobby or advocate for the cause they support or their own financial and organizational interests. The Association for Recreation Management launched some years ago in New York City is but one example. The

149

sector will also address legislative concerns through sector-wide organizations such as the Independent Sector.

Of course, the general public as well as the customers or constituents of nonprofit service providers should be involved in the decision-making process. As consumerism strengthens, there may be job opportunities in that function.

12. NPOs are paying the price of being the source of services of "last resort."

NPOs are often the last organization to step in voluntarily and take responsibility for providing sorely needed services to our citizens in the most difficulty. Often this takes place at a time when society at large has lost interest in these people. As a result, many NPOs may have difficulty securing adequate compensation for the cost of providing such services. As a job seeker, this may mean that your potential employers will be struggling hard for adequate resources that they believe are needed to get the job done. If you have fund raising skills or interests, there are likely to be a number of opportunities.

13. Sophistication among NPO managers is increasing.

This rise in managerial sophistication seems to be taking place across the full range of organizations from the hard core politically active to the most traditional "old line" agencies. This situation offers nothing but good news to you as a job seeker in the nonprofit sector. The old shibboleth that all of the private sector is well managed and all of the nonprofit sector is poorly managed is simply not true. Stereotypes notwithstanding, there are many private sector organizations that could strengthen how they operate (as those of us who have worked for a number of years in the private sector know). And there are many nonprofit organizations that are extremely well managed. Peter Drucker's reported accolade to a nonprofit youth-serving agency as being one of the best run organizations in the United States is but one of many examples of knowledgeable observers identifying nonprofit organizations for their management prowess.

The nonprofit sector is one that has chronically operated with extremely limited resources. Over time a growing premium has been placed on management skill and talent in the sector in order to carry out organizational missions with limited resources. This situation has resulted in a very modest influx of more talented and better trained managers. Of even greater importance, a number of already-in-place, seasoned nonprofit organization managers have sought and acquired increased management skills.

This general upgrading of the management sophistication and talent of the leadership of the nonprofit sector is slowly translating itself into higher standards for executives and staff performance within nonprofit organizations. Boards of directors are also showing renewed interest in better management practice. This is all to the good! The more rational the system, the better chance you will have!

For example this means to a new worker in the sector that there is a growing possibility that the objectives of your organization will become more clear, the personnel will be more fairly managed, and that institutional problems will be addressed more squarely to name just a few of the good things that take place as the sophistication and quality of management practices improve.

To the individual considering a career in the nonprofit sector, there is still a tremendous shortage of highly trained managers in the sector. Should management and/or administration be your interest and/or background, there is still a large gap that you might help fill. There is an even greater need for 'social entrepreneurs' who can link capital with sound, creative program ideas for society's benefit.

NPO managers also need to stay clear about how well they must do tasks which aren't their job. NPOs are so often understaffed that we often wear multiple hats. Don't be afraid to put your shoulder to several wheels, but do your primary responsibilities first . . . and keep the record straight about which jobs are "short-term extra assignments." And remember that you will be best remembered for the tasks you do well rather than the volume of them!

The other implication is that as the management process and the managers themselves become more sophisticated in the nonprofit sector, there will be a growing inclination to accept new or transferred ideas from the public and private sectors for application in the nonprofit sector. And, as new alliances between the sectors are encouraged by the current administration and by the force of limited resources, there will be an increased propensity to reward and promote persons who understand other sectors and how to forge and execute productive alliances with them.

14. There will be greater attention paid to key managerial functions such as strategic planning, financial analysis and managerial control.

There will be new opportunities for sophisticated application of financial and tax analysis of the economic implications of economic development and other finance-oriented projects executed within the context of the nonprofit sector. For example, the work of Santa Monica, California's Ed Kirshner and a number of his nonprofit sector clients in using sophisticated tax shelter-oriented financing mechanisms to generate capital for NPO projects is paving new ground. There will continue to be considerable use of entrepreneurial skills and approaches to nonprofit sector activity. And this entrepreneurial spirit will be much more highly valued within and better understood by NPO boards of directors as the sector matures.[5]

It is a very positive sign that the traditional notions of good work, starvation wages, and "you're on your own" regarding your own career development, appear to be fading somewhat in the sector. Taking their place in a number of quarters are more intelligent and humane personnel management systems, more enlightened and flexible approaches to compensation, increased flexibility in job structure, location and hours, and an increased interest in training and building up the skills of nonprofit employees, to name just a few examples. However, do not believe the picture is all rosy. The notion that the nonprofit employee is able to live on substantial doses of psychic income as opposed to cash and limited or little concern about career development by NPO boards remains alive and well in all too many quarters.

15. Changes in the federal tax codes may hurt the sector.

The course of the current debate over reforms in the federal tax code will shift many times before final decisions are made and implemented. However, as of this writing it appears that some of the propositions may well harm NPOs in the end. As the sector of last resort, the nonprofit sector needs adequate financial (and human) capital to conduct its affairs in a sound manner.

There is growing evidence that to the extent that the deductibility of charitable acts is eliminated or reduced, the sector will be harmed. I suspect that if our congress, other key public officials, and the general public itself better understood the important role of the sector in keeping our society's social fabric strong and whole, there would be less risk of negative-to-the-sector actions taken in the name of tax "reform."

16. The nonprofit sector's independence continues to decline.

As Waldemar Nielsen put it, "The old era of laissez-faire pluralism is . . . beyond any doubt past."[6] Mr. Nielsen sees a new era of far greater interconnection between the three sectors than exists currently. Greg Smith, author and astute observer of the nonprofit sector, also sniffs changes in the wind. He sees a third phase of philanthropy that uses collaboration and social entrepreneurship to far greater degrees than in the past.[7]

The implication for the job seeker is the need to have a wider perspective, especially for senior positions. For example, it will be useful to "speak the language" of several sectors; to have worked in more than one sector; to have contacts in several sectors; and so on.

This new level of interconnectedness also places a higher premium on the job seeker's capacity to conceptualize and then be able to operate within complex interorganizational environments. It also places high values on communication and negotiation skills. For, as Mr. Nielsen indicated, "The frictions arising from the prickliness of the nonprofits and the bureaucratic excesses of government can perhaps be eased to some extent by better training and better procedures."[8] However, we are also likely to see increased regulation and other efforts to encourage greater accountability on the part of institutions in the nonprofit sector.

Finally, there will always be a substantial level of governmental involvement in the nonprofit sector due to four major considerations articulated recently in an Urban Institute paper on "Voluntary Organizations and the Crisis of the Welfare State:"[9]

- Financial—government money will remain a key source since private giving and voluntary activity alone will not be sufficient to maintain the human services our advanced society now requires.
- Equity—government will help ensure a more equitable distribution of limited resources geographically and between population segments.
- Diversity—public funds will help prevent a monopoly by the most established agencies as well as excessive intrusion into citizens' lives by overzealous agencies.
- Public priority-setting—public funds ensure that the general public has a say in which services are delivered and the means of delivery.

17. Appreciation (by society, parents, spouses, children et al.) for the complexity and validity of the work is lacking!

Regrettably for those working or contemplating working in the sector, there still is a relationship between remuneration and status.

Since many NPO jobs are not valued highly by society in general, they can be lower paid. On the other hand, there is some growing evidence (albeit anecdotal in the main) suggesting that NPO workers are making headway in their struggle to be adequately compensated.

It also appears that the self-respect, peer respect, and societal respect for persons working in the nonprofit sector are seriously "out of sync" with one another. This means that the successful job seeker or the happier NPO employee must be fairly clear about his or her own personal needs, skills, and desires. In this sector we still have to develop a reasonably solid sense of self and personal worth and keep clear about our substantial contribution to society, since societal recognition may not be as prevalent or easily forthcoming as those of us who work in the sector might like.

Why does this situation exist? Here are some speculations. First, there is less familiarity in society with the mission and special problems of NPOs. Second, many people assume that lower compensation suggests that the work is less important or less difficult to do. Third, those who do not share or believe in the cause of your particular NPO may not value your work on behalf of that cause, especially if it is generally unpopular. Fourth, work with the poor and disadvantaged is often not valued by society as much as work in the private sector.

On a more positive note, I have also often observed envy on the part of government- or business-sector persons when talking to a nonprofit person. Some of these business and/or government folks wish that their work had a higher "helping others" or "truly important to the quality of life" content. Moreover, the good work of nonprofit sector organizations such as the Council on Foundations, the Independent Sector, the Urban Institute, the United Way of America, and the National Society of Fund Raising Executives to name just a few are helping to change the image of the nonprofit sector by communicating the facts about its vital role in our society.

18. The changing demography and lifestyles of this country will affect the prospects for the nonprofit sector.

Change is accelerating in our society. A number of the expected shifts will impact our society in significant ways. For example:

- The growing proportion of the elderly in the United States will expand jobs in geriatrics and other work with the elderly while shrinking work with young people in relative terms.

- Shifts in the manufacturing segment of the for-profit sector will lead to changes in the priority placed on retraining throughout society, including the nonprofit sector. For example, vocational teachers will be in higher demand as job retraining becomes more necessary and common. Opportunities for entrepreneurial NPOs in this area will grow in the years ahead.
- Continued changes in labor force participation rates of women will lead to a growing need for child care, especially at or near the work place. Fewer volunteers will be available during the work day. The rise in the number of single heads of households will also contribute to the increased demand for child care, though the private sector is likely to move into child care provision fairly aggressively. Continuing interest in health, fitness, and wellness will lead to an emphasis on different, less work-committed lifestyles. Health education will expand and shift further toward a more prevention-oriented mode.
- The growth in the number of people living alone will create opportunities for NPOs to help people form new friendships and develop a sense of belonging and caring.
- Waves of new immigrants will continue to create a demand for expanded services to assist them to move into the mainstream of American life. Language and literacy training will be growth areas.
- The growing strength of articulate, even aggressive religious groups will raise the value and need for new partnerships between religious and nonreligious NPOs. Persons able to deal knowledgeably with both sectors are likely to be in demand.
- Increased work at home through the use of new technologies will expand the need of social and recreational services. It is also likely to decentralize NPOs themselves.
- The competition between nonprofit organizations and private sector businesses may escalate as each sector invades the other's turf in search of additional revenues.
- The need to restore and rebuild the nation's infrastructure in concert with substantial, and economically unproductive commitments to military expenditures will place heavy pressure on the availability of capital for *social* investment. Those who can help "work" the capital markets are likely to have some special opportunities.
- The growth of the nonprofit sector will remain intimately bound up with the maturing of the so-called service economy. Nonprofit-provided services are part of the mix, and most of

the futurists tell us that the service economy is well on its way.[10]

19. The nature of work in the sector will change.

Work in this sector will change in a variety of ways. For example:

- The adoption of more private sector personnel practices will increase the use of incentive compensation and more vigorous personnel evaluation.
- There will be both expanded opportunities for and increased limitations on volunteers. As more people, especially women, attempt to enter the work force or take second jobs, the pool of volunteers and the number of volunteer hours may decline. On the other hand the priority given to management and exchange between sectors will expand volunteer involvement opportunities.
- Staff loads are likely to grow in many NPOs as budget cuts take hold and demand for services grows.
- There is likely to be some growth in the "high-tech" aspects of nonprofit sector work (i.e., more computer applications, expanded use of biotechnology, etc.) but not nearly as much growth as many expect. In fact, some estimates suggest that only one in twenty-five new jobs are now expected to be "technology-oriented."[11] This modest technological growth may not provide lots of new jobs but will be very important to individual organizations either maintaining a competitive edge or surviving. Such skills are also likely to be important to the individual's development, growth, and success.
- Growing automation of many aspects of our society and the increased use of electronic data processing (EDP) equipment will also increase the demand in this predominantly service sector for those who are adept at dealing with other people. A similar demand will exist for those who are good at helping facilitate and execute the solving of interpersonal problems.
- Continued growth of litigiousness will lead to a higher demand for those with good mediation and dispute resolution skills.

Note that while it is useful to grasp likely future trends, one should not be afraid to ignore some of them as well. If Michael Jackson or his brothers had looked too closely at the number of openings for singers, they might never have launched their careers.

20. Sanctimonious attitudes can be potentially corrosive.

There is a risk in this sector of catching the virus of self-importance, the feeling that this sector's work is more important, more relevant, more useful than that of the other sectors. Excessive pride can cause us to forget that the power that drives the nonprofit engines comes from a combination of the savings of individuals and their charitable instincts, profits from our whole economy, and tax revenues generated by the government from the private sector.

Moreover, there are many opportunities to do "high social content" work in both the profit and government sectors. It may be that there will be greater opportunities and more challenging positions for you by introducing your "nonprofit concerns" to the other two sectors. Many progressive corporate leaders have done so by bringing some substance to the concept of corporate social responsibility.* Thousands of other dedicated corporate people apply the know how and financial/material resources of their companies to tough social problems every day.

21. The long-term career opportunities, at least in some subsegments, can be somewhat limited.

Some elements of the nonprofit sector are stable (some would say stagnant) industries. They are not growing. This means that the only new jobs come with retirements and people resigning or being terminated. Low turnover can slow down or eliminate promotion opportunities. For example, a number of universities are losing some of their best potential future instructors because there is such limited turnover.

Some other elements of the sector are declining because of shifts or reductions in federal support of the sector. For example, the current administration has shifted spending through the first half of the 1980s toward older Americans and away from children's services. This will reduce job opportunities in children's services and expand them in the field of services to the elderly. Other elements of the sector likely to expand include home health care and intermediary organizations in large metropolitan areas. And, self-help organizations are likely to

---

* There is a substantial literature treating corporate social responsibility by authors such as Clark Abt, Kirke Hanson, David Johnston, David Linnowes, Prakesh Sethi and myself to name just a few samples. Some of us have also addressed corporate social policy in the international/transnational context.

continue to endure and grow, though there will be substantial peaks and valleys in the pattern.

Thus, it may be beneficial for young people entering some of the subfields, such as philanthropy, to plan to move in and out to ensure that they continue to grow and have adequate challenge and maintain some upward mobility. One strategy is to plan to spend a few years, on at least one occasion, working in the private or public sectors, adding to your skills and expanding both your base of experience and contacts. Multisectoral experience can increase your value in the non-profit sector and strengthen your own experience base.

22. The advent of the "new national narcissism" may erode voluntary efforts and support of the nonprofit sector.

The third sector thrives best in times of a substantial spirit of compassion and community. If it becomes more prevalent, a formidable opponent could be "the 'new narcissism,' that 'is a national obsession with things having to do with self-fulfillment, self-betterment and self-enhancement to the exclusion of an awareness of others, of investment in community, to a valuing of our collective existence."[12]

23. Nonprofit organizations will become increasingly important in the career development of those segments of our society which have historically had less-than-full access to employment opportunity.

Some NPOs will address this issue as their primary function. Many of the rest will recognize that there is a considerable amount of untapped human capital available to the sector. By giving greater attention to training and human resource development, the sector will be able to use effectively a relatively untapped resource in this country.

24. A growing number of NPOs will adopt international agendas.

As the world shrinks and the intertwined character of the world's countries emerges there are likely to be increased opportunities to work on international issues here or abroad.

* * *

These are just a few examples of the changes in the wind that will affect the nonprofit sector. I encourage you to talk to knowledgeable people in greater depth about the changes coming in that segment of the sector that interests you most. It will strengthen your ability to interview well and, more important, provide a strong background for you to understand better the context of your sector.

Notes
Chapter 8

1. Nielsen, *Endangered Sector,* 186.

2. Lester M. Salamon, "Nonprofits: The Results are Coming In," *Foundation News,* July/August 1984, 18.

3. Lester M. Salamon (Speech at the Nonprofit Management Association Annual Conference, San Francisco, 6 June 1984).

4. Nielsen,*Endangered Sector,* 186.

5. For a thorough analysis of entrepreneurs in the nonprofit sector see Dennis R. Young, *If Not for Profit, What? A Behavioral Theory of the Nonprofit Sector Based on Entrepreneurship* (Lexington, Mass.: Lexington Books, 1983).

6. Nielsen, *Endangered Sector,* 187.

7. See Smith's forthcoming book, *Philanthropy Three,* to be published this year.

8. Nielsen, *Endangered Sector,* 199.

9. Lester M. Salamon, James C. Musslewhite, Jr., and Alan J. Abramson, *Voluntary Organizations and the Crisis of the Welfare State* (Washington, D.C.:The Urban Institute, October 1983), 26.

10. "What Lies Ahead—A Mid-Decade View," a United Way of America report, provides further detail on several of the topics cited in this section. Copies of the report are available from Mr. Steve Delfin, Director, Public Relations, United Way of America, 701 N. Fairfax St., Alexandria, Va. 22314-2045.

11. John U. Burgan of the Bureau of Labor Statistics as quoted in *New York Times,* 14 October 1984, Section 12, p. 6.

12. Michael R. Ostrowski, "The Third Sector: From Definition to Purpose and Policy" (Paper prepared for University of Colorado at Denver doctoral program, 3 July 1985), 22.

Conclusion

You are in good hands now—your own. Although a book such as this one can provide information, resources, tips, and techniques, it cannot fully guarantee success. Only you can achieve the ultimate goal of securing a nonprofit organization job and launching a nonprofit career. Only you can take this information and create the strategy for your search, a strategy that will take some time and effort, if it is to be fruitful.

I invite you to write me c/o my publisher, The Taft Group, 5130 MacArthur Blvd. NW, Washington, DC 20016 with your suggestions and comments on *Careers in the Nonprofit Sector*. I would love to hear from you on how this book was helpful or how it could be improved.

Finally, good luck in your search. Countless others have made it, I know you can too. Continue to explore, to seek out new contacts and experiences, and you will find the situation that's right for you. And when you do, I only wish for you the enjoyment from your nonprofit career that I am deriving from mine.

Terry W. McAdam
Malibu, California
September, 1986

Appendix A

A SAMPLE FROM THE LARGER 501(C)-DESIGNATED ORGANIZATIONS BY FIELD OF INTEREST

The list below of 501(c)-designated organizations was selected from the most recent data available at time of preparation, a 1984 compilation of the 1,000 largest such organizations by operating budget. It was prepared by the Taft Group and is a random selection made from that compilation to illustrate not the largest NPOs but the diversity of NPOs within that group of the 1,000 largest nonprofit organizations. In this appendix, they are presented alphabetically within nine major categories. The organizations were compiled from among the twenty-three 501(c) designations of the Internal Revenue Service (for more information on these and three additional classifications of tax-exempt organizations, see IRS Publication 557 *Tax-Exempt Status for Your Organization*).

Arts and Humanities

Colonial Williamsburg Foundation, Williamsburg, VA
Corporation for Public Broadcasting, Washington, DC
Henry E. Huntington Library & Art Gallery, San Marino, CA
Metropolitan Museum of Art, New York, NY
Motion Picture and Television Fund, Woodland Hills, CA
New York Shakespeare Festival, New York, NY
Smithsonian Institution, Washington, DC
Walker Art Center, Inc., Minneapolis, MN

Associations and Special Interests

American Association of Retired Persons, Long Beach, CA
American Cotton Growers, Lubbock, TX
American Management Association, New York, NY
American Medical Association, Chicago, IL
Danish Creamery Association, Fresno, CA
Federation of Jewish Philanthropies of New York, New York, NY
International Alliance of Theatrical Stage Employees, Studio City, CA
International Brotherhood of Teamsters Chauffeurs, Washington, DC
Livestock Producers Cooperative Association, Columbus, OH
Los Angeles Olympic Organizing Committee, Los Angeles, CA
Michigan Livestock Exchange, Manchester, MI
Mountain Empire Dairymen's Association, Inc., Thornton, CO
Producers Marketing Association, Inc., Indianapolis, IN
Sunkist Growers, Inc., Van Nuys, CA

Sunsweet Growers, Inc., Stockton, CA
Transport Workers Union of New York City, New York, NY
United Brotherhood of Carpenters & Joiners of America, Washington, DC
United Jewish Appeal of Greater New York, Inc., New York, NY
United Steelworkers of America, Pittsburgh, PA

Education

Baylor College of Medicine, Houston, TX
Catholic University of America, Washington, DC
Chicago College of Osteopathic Medicine, Chicago, IL
College Entrance Examination Board, New York, NY
Drexel University, Philadelphia, PA
Educational Broadcasting Corporation, New York, NY
Educational Testing Service, Princeton, NJ
Gallaudet College, Washington, DC
Howard University, Washington, DC
Johns Hopkins University, Baltimore, MD
Kansas University Endowment Association, Lawrence, KS
Loma Linda University, Loma Linda, CA
Michigan Education Special Services Association, East Lansing, MI
National Education Association of the United States, Washington, DC
President & Fellows of Harvard College, Cambridge, MA
Rensselaer Polytechnic Institute, Troy, NY
Rochester Institute of Technology, Rochester, NY
St. Paul's School, Concord, NH
Temple University, Philadelphia, PA
Trustees of Iowa College-Grinnell, IA
Trustees of Princeton University, Princeton, NJ
University of Denver Colorado Seminary, Denver, CO
Wayne State University, Detroit, MI

Financial (Assets or Benefits)

Aid Association for Lutherans, Appleton, WI
Arizona State Carpenters Health & Welfare Trust Fund, Phoenix, AZ
Boilermakers National Health & Welfare Fund, Kansas City, KS
Caterpillar Tractor Co. Group Insurance Trust, Peoria, IL
Credit Union Department of the State of Texas, Austin, TX
Hewlett-Packard Company Employee Benefits Organization, Palo Alto, CA
Montgomery Ward & Co., Inc. Comprehensive Health Care, Chicago, IL
Social Insurance Plan of Bethlehem Steel Corporation, Bethlehem, PA
Teachers Insurance and Annuity Association of America, New York, NY
Trans-Alaska Pipeline Liability Fund, Anchorage, AK
United States Letter Carriers Mutual Benefit Association, Washington, DC
Young Men's Christian Association Retirement Fund, New York, NY

Foundations, Trusts

Alton Ochsner Medical Foundation, New Orleans, LA
Anne Burnett Tandy and Charles Tandy Foundation, Fort Worth, TX
Arthur S. Demoss Foundation, Chattanooga, TN
Cannon Foundation, Inc., Concord, NC
Ford Foundation, New York, NY
Foundation for Economic Education, Inc., Irvington, NY
Fred Meyer Charitable Trust, Portland, OR
G. Harold and Leila Mathers Charitable Foundation, White Plains, NY
J. Paul Getty Trust, Los Angeles, CA
John M. Olin Foundation, Inc., New York, NY
Lovelace Medical Foundation, Albuquerque, NM
Mayo Foundation, Rochester, MN
McKnight Foundation, Minneapolis, MN
Meadows Foundation, Inc., Dallas, TX
Nemours Foundation, Jacksonville, FL
Richard King Mellon Foundation, Pittsburgh, PA
Robert Wood Johnson Foundation, Princeton, NJ
University of Minnesota Foundation, Minneapolis, MN
W. Alton Jones Foundation, Inc., Charlottesville, VA
W. K. Kellogg Foundation Trust, Chicago, IL

Health

Albert Einstein Medical Center, Philadelphia, PA
American Cancer Society, Inc., New York, NY
American Red Cross, Washington, DC
Blue Cross & Blue Shield, Omaha, NE
Blue Cross of Central New York, Inc., Syracuse, NY
Blue Shield of Georgia, Columbus, GA
Blue Shield of Massachusetts, Inc., Boston, MA
California Physicians Service, San Francisco, CA
Childrens Hospital of Philadelphia, Philadelphia, PA
Deaconess Hospital of Cleveland, Cleveland, OH
District Nursing Association of Fall River, Inc., Fall River, MA
Holy Cross Hospital of Silver Spring, Inc., Silver Spring, MD
Intermountain Health Care, Inc., Salt Lake City, UT
Mobile Infirmary Association, Mobile, AL
Muscular Dystrophy Association, Inc., New York, NY
Nassau Hospital Association, Mineola, NY
North Mississippi Medical Center, Tupelo, MS
Pierce County Medical Bureau, Inc., Tacoma, WA
St. Francis Hospital and Medical Center, Hartford, CT
St. Vincent's Medical Center, Bridgeport, CT
Swedish Hospital Medical Center, Seattle, WA
Xerox Employees Medical Care Plan, Xerox Corporation, Stamford, CT

Religious

Billy Graham Evangelistic Association, Minneapolis, MN
Campus Crusade for Christ, Inc., San Bernardino, CA
Church Charity Foundation of Long Island, Hempstead, NY
Religious Communities Trust, Chicago, IL
Sisters of Charity of Nazareth, Nazareth, KY

Research

Advertising Research Foundation, Inc., New York, NY
American Petroleum Institute, Washington, DC
Gas Research Institute, Chicago, IL
IIT Research Institute, Chicago, IL
National Geographic Society, Washington, DC
Research Medical Center, Kansas City, MO
Scripps Clinic & Research Foundation, La Jolla, CA
University Research Association, Washington, DC

Social Services

Boy Scouts of America National Council, Irving, TX
Cooperative for American Relief Everywhere, Inc., New York, NY
Girl Scouts of the United States of America, New York, NY
Knouse Foods Cooperative, Inc., Peach Glen, PA
Lycoming County Commission for Community Action, Williamsport, PA
Mercer Street Friends Center, Trenton, NJ
Milan Volunteer Fire Department, Inc., Rhinebeck, NY
National Rural Utilities Cooperative Finance Corporation, Washington, DC
Rotary Foundation of Rotary International, Evanston, IL
South Dakota Housing Development Authority, Pierre, SD
United Way, Inc., Los Angeles, CA

Appendix B

SELF-TEST FOR COMPATIBILITY WITH THE NONPROFIT SECTOR

Instructions: Make a copy of the following and write out appropriate ratings for yourself for each of the characteristics/traits. There is neither a quantitative scoring system nor a right or wrong answer. By thoughtfully exploring how you feel about each characteristic and trait you will begin to develop a broad and rich sense of your compatibility with many of the different aspects of life in the sector.

The point here is to provide you with a both general map and a disciplined approach to begin to think about a number of highly qualitative aspects of the sector.[1]

---

[1]Several of the skills, attitudes, and attributes of the successful individual in the nonprofit sector have been identified by Brian O'Connell, President, Independent Sector, in, for example, "Effective Sector Leadership," Keynote Address, Professional Education Forum, *Independent Sector*, 31 October 1984, Washington, D.C., or "It Takes a 'Different Animal' to Succeed, in Nonprofit Management . . . ." *The Nonprofit Executive*, Taft Group, June 1983.

Sector Characteristics/Traits

	A Few Sentences About How I Feel/Rate/Stack Up

Skills

- Relating well to people (in general)

- Relating well to a lot of different types of people.

- Ingenuity in use of available (read limited) resources

- Substantial flexibility in adapting to changing circumstances

- Capacity to self-start and be entrepreneurial without the big financial rewards which come to private sector entrepreneurs

- Ability to enlist cooperation of others without total hierarchical control

- Able to motivate people via other than financial incentives

- Have high degree of energy

Attitudes and Values

- Enjoy helping others

- Am self-motivated

- Have a firm commitment to public service

- Have a fair amount of sympathy and empathy for others

- Willing to work with and through others

- Don't expect to "get rich quick"

- Have reasonable tolerance for both ambiguity and complex problems

- Able to operate well in relatively unstructured work environment

- Don't have to have direct feedback (some of helping professions get lots, however)

- Willing to advocate for others and the sector

- Can subordinate many of my personal needs and preferences to those of volunteer leadership/board

169

Sector Characteristics/Traits	A Few Sentences About How I Feel/Rate/Stack Up
• Am flexible (will face higher than average need to adapt and change schedules, find creative approaches to new problems, deal with changes in resources or whatever)	
• Am tolerant of variety of views and approaches	
• Reasonable level of patience—but some sector people are also good if they are change agents (agents provocateurs)	
• Willing to work hard	
• Am mature—able to forego short-term satisfactions for the attainment of long-term goals. Satisfaction doesn't always (often?) come measured in days, weeks, or even months	
• Am persistent, can pursue a goal despite long-time frame and mixed progress measures.	

Appendix C

EDUCATION AND TRAINING OPPORTUNITIES

In keeping with the intent of this book to provide you a guide and methodical approach to your search, this appendix lists a number of resources available for information on educational and training opportunities.

DIRECTORIES AND NEWSLETTERS

*Resource Directory of Education
and Training Opportunities*
The Independent Sector
1828 L Street, NW
Washington, DC 20036

$18.00, prepaid only. This excellent directory lists over 500 educational programs available from universities, institutes, consultants, and organizations in 39 states and Canada, as well as sources of financial aid, consulting services, and training facilities.

The Taft Nonprofit Executive
The Taft Group
5130 MacArthur Boulevard, NW
Washington, DC 20016

$97/year, published monthly, includes "NPE Careers," a positions available/ wanted section for opportunities across the sector and nation.

LOCAL COLLEGES AND UNIVERSITIES

Increasingly, postsecondary institutions are offering full-time, degree-level, and continuing education courses, workshops, and seminars for the nonprofit field that can result in a degree or certificate. Subject topics to look under in their course catalogs include:

- executive development
- human resources administration
- marketing for nonprofit organizations
- policy planning
- public administration
- volunteer program administration

Colleges and universities are also the sites of conferences and symposia; keep·an eye out for posted notices, announcements in the campus paper, or coverage in your local paper.

LOCAL "OPEN" OR "FREE" UNIVERSITIES, CULTURAL INSTITUTIONS

Such programs, often found in major metropolitan areas, are sometimes a source of low-cost exposure to the milieu of the nonprofit sector. Some examples:

Open University
3333 Connecticut Avenue, NW
Washington, DC 20008

Resident Associate Activities Program
Smithsonian Institution
Washington, DC 20560

The Learning Tree University
1408 Thousand Oaks Boulevard
Thousand Oaks, CA 91362

NATIONAL NONPROFIT ORGANIZATIONS

These organizations often offer training seminars, programs, and workshops sometimes just to members and sometimes to the public. Examples of these types of organization are:

- United Way
- YMCA, YWCA, YMHA, YWHA
- Girl Scouts of the U.S.A.
- U.S. Chamber of Commerce.

TRAINING AND ADVOCACY INSTITUTES AND ORGANIZATIONS

VOLUNTEER–The National Center
1111 North 19th Street
Arlington, VA 22209

Institute for Nonprofit Organization Management
University of Colorado
518 17th Street
Denver, CO 80202

Institute for Nonprofit Organization Management
College of Professional Studies
University of San Francisco
Ignatian Heights
San Francisco, CA 94117-1080

Southern California Center for Nonprofit Management
1052 W. Sixth Street, Suite 700
Los Angeles, CA 90017

PROFESSIONAL ASSOCIATIONS

Both management and nonprofit associations of professionals offer courses, seminars, training, and sometimes certification or job banks. Some examples of these associations follow. Appendix G offers an expanded list of similar and "umbrella"-type organizations that also have additional information.

American Society of Association Executives
1575 Eye Street, NW
Washington, DC 20005

National Society of Fund Raising Executives
1101 King Street, Suite 300
Alexandria, VA 22314

Nonprofit Management Association
Box 2350
Minneapolis, MN 55402

Association of Part-Time Professionals
7655 Old Springhouse Road
McLean, VA 22102

EMPLOYMENT SEARCH/ASSISTANCE SERVICES

Many such services are springing up that cater exclusively to the nonprofit sector. If you're already in the nonprofit sector, you may wish to explore this possibility; as always when purchasing such services, caveat emptor! *Fund Raising Management,* a leading magazine in the field, is one source of advertised services, generally firms looking to place experienced people. The National Society of Fund Raising Executives has a career service for its members; umbrella organizations often have job hotlines, and your local Yellow Pages is another source.

TRANSITION (clergy in career change)
2000 Aldrich Avenue South
Minneapolis, MN 55405
(612) 874-0104

OPTIONS—A program arranged through the synods, bishops of the American Lutheran Church, the Association of Evangelical Lutheran Churches, and The Lutheran Church in America. See chapter 6 for more information.

See also Action Step 32 of Chapter 5.

Appendix D

GEOGRAPHIC INDEX TO PEOPLE INTERVIEWED IN CHAPTER 4

ARKANSAS
Hampton, Cronin, Jerry. Project Manager, Independent Community Consultants, Inc.

CALIFORNIA
Los Angeles, Farner, Saralei. Office Manager, Southern California Center for Nonprofit Management

Los Angeles, MacFarland, Kee. Director, Child Sexual Abuse Diagnostic Center, Children's Institute International

San Diego, Quan, Phyllis. Partner, D'Agostino, Underwood, Quan and Associates

San Francisco, Layton, Tom. Executive Director, Wallace Alexander Gerbode Foundation

COLORADO
Denver, Leduc, Robert. Executive Director, Anshutz Family Foundation

Boulder, Welsh, Joan. Executive Director, Boulder County Safehouse

MINNESOTA
Minneapolis, Barreiro, Terri. Director of Planning, Allocations and evaluation, the United Way of the Minneapolis Area

St. Paul, Himmelman, Arthur. Associate Director, McKnight Foundation

NEW YORK
New York, Dumpson, James R. Vice President, New York Community Trust

WASHINGTON, DC
Roisman, Lois. Executive Director, Jewish Fund for Justice

Appendix E

THE JOB CHANGE WORKSHEET*

This potential job change worksheet provides you with a mechanical tool to help you take a first cut at whether you should be thinking more about changing jobs. Here are a few of the questions you might ask yourself about your situation. Answer each with a check (√). I'll suggest an approach to interpreting the results at the end, but the greatest value to you is the process of thinking through carefully each question which will provide some clue about whether you should begin to think more seriously about leaving your present organization before you do so!

I. 1. Look at the financial health of the organization you are contemplating leaving.
Your rating: Very Poor   Poor   Satisfactory   Good   Very Good

2. How much turnover takes place?
Your rating: Very Poor   Poor   Satisfactory   Good   Very Good

3. What is the general mood and morale of the place? Do people who work there seem to enjoy it?
Your rating: Very Poor   Poor   Satisfactory   Good   Very Good

4. What is your sense of the communications environment?
A. Are doors open?
Your rating: Very Poor   Poor   Satisfactory   Good   Very Good

B. Are meetings held often enough to facilitate communication?
Your rating: Very Poor   Poor   Satisfactory   Good   Very Good

C. Do people seem to know what is generally going on in the organization?
Your rating: Very Poor   Poor   Satisfactory   Good   Very Good

D. Do people seem supportive of one another?

Your rating: Very Poor   Poor   Satisfactory   Good   Very Good

---

* Most of these measures were adopted from chapter 6 of Srully T. Blotnick, *The Corporate Steeplechase, Predictable Crises in a Business Career* Facts on File, New York: 1984

II. 5. If you have been invited to work elsewhere:

A. Is the new organization's financial health:

Your rating: Very Poor   Poor   Satisfactory   Good   Very Good

B. Are you able to get a feel about the overall health of the work atmosphere from people you know (or can get to know) who work there now?

Your rating: Very Poor   Poor   Satisfactory   Good   Very Good

C. Is the specific division, section, or part of the nonprofit known to you—and healthy?

Your rating: Very Poor   Poor   Satisfactory   Good   Very Good

III. 6. If you give up your current position and the new one doesn't work out:

A. Will you be significantly worse off than you are now?

Your answer: Yes   Not Sure   No

B. Do you have some concrete ideas about a fallback position and the resources to sustain you until you can secure it?

Your answer: Yes   Not Sure   No

HOW TO INTERPRET YOUR ANSWERS

After you have answered all the questions as honestly as you can, go back and look at your answers graphically. If your check marks in Part I are all to the left of the page while to the right of the page in Part II, then a job change may be indicated. If the check marks seem evenly distributed, then careful thought is needed regarding the risks you're willing to take and the tradeoffs you're willing to make. Finally, the answers to the questions in Part III will serve as swing factors; obviously, you won't take a new job if you'll be worse off, regardless of your answers, and a fallback position may not be necessary. (Although I would suggest that it is unless you are independently wealthy!) Please recognize that this worksheet is just a thought starter.

Also remember those other old tried (and true) maxims:

● Work should not be *everything* in your life.

● The grass always looks greener on the other side of the fence.

Appendix F

FURTHER READING ABOUT THE SECTOR AND FINDING WORK IN IT

In addition to the references cited within and at the end of each chapter, the following selections are given as books that provide further insight on the nonprofit sector and the work and jobs available in it. There are two parts, On the Nonprofit Sector and On Finding Careers in the Sector. Some titles may no longer be in print, but you should be able to find them at your library. References are listed alphabetically by title.

ON THE NONPROFIT SECTOR

A Communications Manual for Nonprofit Organizations. Maddalena, Lucille A. New York, AMACOM, 1981.

A Window on the World of Philanthropy, A Compilation of Insights. Doherty, Elizabeth M., Kliefoth, Lisa H., and Singer, Elizabeth A. Washington, D.C., Council of Better Business Bureaus, 1984.

America's Voluntary Spirit. O'Connell, Brian. New York, The Foundation Center, 1983, p. 1.

Arts Money: Raising It, Saving It and Earning It. Jeffri. Joan. New York, New York, Neal-Schuman Publishers, Inc., 1983.

Budgeting for Nonprofit Organizations. Vinler, Robert D., and Kish, Rhea K. New York, New York. The Free Press, a Division of Macmillan, Inc., 1984.

Charity U.S.A. Bakal, Carl. New York, Times Books, 1979.

Corporate Philanthropy. Washington, D.C., Council on Foundations, 1982.

"Corporate Philanthropy—An Integral Part of Corporate Social Responsibility." *Business Roundtable.* March 1981.

Corporate Philanthropy in America: New Perspectives for the Eighties. Lord, Benjamin. Washington, D.C., The Taft Group, 1984.

"Corporate Social Responsibility—A New Term for an Old Concept with New Significance." Haas, Walter A., Jr. In *Corporations and Their Critics: Issues and Answers to the Problems of Corporate Responsibility,* edited by Thornton Bradshaw and David Vogel. New York, McGraw-Hill, 1982.

Effective Leadership in Voluntary Organizations. O'Connell, Brian, New York, New York, Association Press, 1976.

Enterprise in the Nonprofit Sector. Crimmins, James C. and Keil, Mary. New York, New York and Washington, D.C., Partners for Livable Places and The Rockefeller Brothers Fund, 1983.

Excellence; Can We Be Equal and Excellent Too? Gardner, John W. New York, W. W. Norton & Company, 1984.

Foundations, Private Giving, and Public Policy, Report and Recommendations of the Commission on Foundations and Private Philanthropy. Chicago, Illinois. The University of Chicago Press, 1970.

Giving and Volunteering: New Froniters of Knowledge. 1985 Spring Research Forum Working Papers, Washington, D.C. Independent Sector and United Way Institute, 1985.

Giving USA. American Association of Fund-Raising Counsel, Inc. Annual Report 1985, New York.

Healing America: What Can Be Done About the Continuing Economic Crisis. Cornuelle, Richard C. New York, G.P. Putnam's Sons, 1983.

How to Rate Your Development Office: A Fund Raising Primer for the Chief Executive. Berendt, Robert J. and Taft, J. Richard, Washington, D.C., The Taft Group, 1984.

How to Manage a Nonprofit Organization. Fisher, John, Toronto, Canada, Management and Fund Raising Centre, 1978.

"How to Serve on a Hospital Board." Underwood, J.M. *Harvard Business Review,* July-August 1969.

If Not For Profit, What? A Behavioral Theory of the Nonprofit Sector Based on Entrepreneurship. Young, Dennis R. Lexington, Massachusetts, Lexington Books, 1983.

"It Takes a 'Different Animal' to Succeed in Nonprofit Management." O'Connell, Brian. *The Nonprofit Executive,* Washington, D.C., The Taft Group, 1983 p. 3,4.

Journal of Voluntary Action Research. Volume 14, Nos. 1-3, January-September 1985. Van Til, Jon, ed., Camden, New Jersey, 1985.

Major Challenges to Philanthropy. Payton, Robert L., (Washington, D.C. A discussion paper for Independent Sector, 1984.

Managing Nonprofit Organizations. Borst, Diane and Montana, Patrick J., ed., New York, New York, AMACOM, 1977.

"Managing Voluntary Associations for the 1980's." Fulmer, Robert M. *Journal of Voluntary Action Research 2,* No. 4 (1973), 212-215.

Management Control in Nonprofit Organizations. Anthony, Robert N. and Heazlinger, Regina. Homewood. Homewood, Illinois, Richard D. Irwin, Inc., 1975 (Note: A later revised edition with a change in authors is now available).

"Nonprofit Organizations and the Rise of Third-Party Government: The Scope, Character, and Consequences of Government Support of Nonprofit Organizations." Salamon, Lester M. Research paper presented at Independent Sector Research Forum, 1983, May 3.

"Personal and Organizational Renewal," Gardner, John W. Speech before the 36th Annual Meeting of the Conference of Southwest Foundations, Fort Worth, Texas, 5 April 1984.

Philanthropy, Voluntary Action, and the Public Good, 1986 Spring Research Forum Working Papers. Washington, D.C., Independent Sector and United Way Institute, 1986.

Private Foreign Aid: U.S. Philanthropy for Relief and Development. Bolling, Landrum R. Boulder, Colorado, Westview Press, 1982.

"Private Philanthropy and Public Needs: Historical Perspective." Bremner, Robert H. In *Research Papers of the Commission on Private Philanthropy and Public Needs*. Vol. 1. Washington, D.C., Department of Treasury, 1977.

Productivity in Service Organizations, Organizing for People. Heaton, Herbert. New York, New York, McGraw-Hill Book Company, 1977.

Servant Leadership. Greenleaf, Robert K. New York, Paulist Press, 1977.

Sleeping Giant: Arousing Church Power in America. Hudnut, Robert K. New York, Harper & Row, 1971.

Strategic Marketing for Nonprofit Organizations, Program and Resource Development. Lauffer, Armand. New York, New York, The Free Press, A Division of MacMillan Inc., 1984.

The Board Members Book, Making A Difference in Voluntary Organizations. O'Connell, Brian. New York, New York. The Foundation Center, 1985.

"The Changing Role of Private Philanthropy in Health Affairs." Blendon, Robert H. In *Research Papers of the Commission on Private Philanthropy and Public Needs*. Vol. 2. Washington, D.C., Department of Treasury, 1977.

"The Crisis of the Nonprofits." Neilsen, Waldemar A. *Change*, January 1980.

The Endangered Sector. Nielsen, Waldemar A. New York, Columbia University Press, 1979.

"The Invisible Partnership, Government and the Nonprofit Sector." Salamon, Lester. *Bell Atlantic Quarterly*, No. 1, Autumn 1984.

The New Corporate Philanthropy. Koch, Frank. New York, Plenum Press, 1979.

The Nonprofit Management Bibliography. Cronin, Jerry, McAdam, Terry W., Jackson, Michael R., and Anthes, Earl W. Minneapolis, Minnesota, The Nonprofit Management Association, 1984.

The Nonprofit Organization Handbook. Conners, Tracy D., ed. New York, McGraw-Hill, 1980.

"The Scope of the Private Voluntary Charitable Sector." Rudney, Gabriel G. In *Research Papers of the Commission on Private Philanthropy and Public Needs*. Vol. 1, Washington, D.C., Department of Treasury, 1977.

The Successful Volunteer Organization. Flanagan, Joan. Chicago, Contemporary Books, Inc., 1981.

179

The Third Sector: Keystone of a Caring Society. Nielsen, Waldemar A. Occasional Paper, No. 1. Washington, D.C., Independent Sector, 1980.

The Thirteen Most Common Fund-Raising Mistakes and How To Avoid Them. Schneiter, Paul H. and Nelson, Donald T. Washington, D.C. The Taft Group, 1982.

Very Nice Work If You Can Get It: The Socially Useful Production Debate. ed. Collective Design Projects. Spokesman, Nottingham, England, 1986.

Voluntary Agencies in the Welfare State. Kramer, Ralph M. Berkeley, California, University of California Press, 1981.

Why Charity? The Care For A Third Sector. Douglas, James D. Sage Publications, Beverly Hills, California, 1983, p. 15.

"Work and Workforce Characteristics in the Nonprofit Sector." Miruis, Philip H. and Hackett, Edward J. *Monthly Labor Review,* U.S. Department of Labor, Bureau of Labor Statistics, April 1983. p. 3-12.

ON FINDING CAREERS IN THE SECTOR

This section contains books and articles you may also find useful. If you don't find what you want here, one of the most comprehensive bibliographies of career books is contained in appendix B of Richard Bolles' *What Color is Your Parachute?* noted below. Further, Impact Publications (Careers Dept., 10655 Big Oak Circle, Manassas, VA 22111) offers a catalog of over 800 job search and career titles. Thanks are due Dr. Lisa Raufman, Moorpark College, for permission to use some of the entries (∗) from her annotated Career Search Bibliography.

1985 Foundation Compensation Report. Joseph, James A., Bons, Elizabeth T., Hooper, Carol A. Washington, D.C., Council on Foundations, 1985.

A Guide to Professional Development Opportunities for College and University Administrators: Seminars, Workshops, Conferences, Institutes and Internships. Washington, D.C., American Council on Education.

Americans Volunteer. Manpower/Automation Research Monograph, No. 10. Washington, D.C., U.S. Department of Labor, 1969.

Career and Life Planning. Moorpark College staff. Moorpark College.∗

Career Patterns in Philanthropy, Odendahl, Teresa; Boris, Elizabeth; Daniels, Arlene K. New York, Russell Sage, 1984.

Dictionary of Occupational Titles. Washington, D.C., U.S. Government Printing Office, 1977.

"Differences in Importance of Job Facts Between Managers in Voluntary and Profit Organizations." Gatewood, Robert and Lahiff, James. *Journal of Voluntary Action Research 6,* No. 3-4 (1977): 133-138.

Directory of Executive Recruiters. Fitzwilliam, N.H., Consultants News.

Employee Benefits for Part-Timers. Rothberg, Diane and Cook, Barbara. McLean, Virginia, Association of Part-Time Professionals, 1985.

"Finding Work With Grantmakers." Campi, Suzanne and McAdam, Terry W. Unpublished monograph, Southern California Association for Philanthropy, Los Angeles, 1984.

Getting To Yes. Negotiating Agreement Without Giving In. Fisher, Roger and Vry, William. New York, Penguin Books, 1983.

Good Works: A Guide to Careers in Social Change. Anzalone, Joan. December 1985.

Guerrilla Tactics in the Job Market. Jackson, Tom. Bantam Books.*

Guide to American Directories. Coral Springs, Florida, B. Klein Publications, 1986.

Hardball Job Hunting Tactics. Wright, Richard. New York, Facts on File, 1983.

"Helpful Hints for a Happy Job Change." Cohen, Joyce. *New York Times,* 10/14/84, Section 12, p. 49.

How to Beat the Employment Game. Moer, David. Ten Speed Press, Berkeley, California.*

I Can Be Anything. Mitchell, Joyce S. Bantam Books.*

Interview! The Executive's Guide to Selecting the Right Personnel. New York, Hastings House Publishers, 1970.

Jobs and Careers for the 80s. Catalog of over 700 career resources. Manassas, Virginia, Impact Publications.

Job Power. Bugg, Ralph. Pyramid Books.*

Job Sharing: Analyzing The Cost. Olmstead, Barney, Smith, Suzzane, and New Ways to Work Job Sharing Project. New Ways to Work, San Francisco, California, 1981.*

Job Sharing: General Information. Olmstead, Barney, Smith, Suzzane, and New Ways to Work Job Sharing Project. New Ways to Work, San Francisco, California, 1982.*

Manager's Guide to Successful Job Hunting Traxel, Robert G. New York, McGraw-Hill, 1978.

Making It On Your First Job When You're Young, Inexperienced, & Ambitious. Schmidt, Peggy J. Avon Books, New York, NY, 1981.

Moving Up. Djeddah, Eli. Ten Speed Press, Berkeley, California.*

"Nonprofit Organizations Offer Profitable Work." Reckson, Alyse. *The New York Times,* 16 October 1983.

Occupational Outlook Handbook. Washington, D.C., U.S. Department of Labor.

Part-Time Professional. Rothberg, Diane and Cook, Barbara. McLean, Virginia, Association of Part-Time Professionals, 1985.

Part-Time Work: A Bibliography. Second edition. Levin, Amy, ed. McLean, Virginia, Association of Part-Time Professionals, 1984.

Parting Company: How to Survive the Loss of a Job and Find Another Successfully. Morin, William H. and Cabrera, James C. New York, Harcourt Brace Jovanovich, 1982, p. 247 ff.

Put Your Degree to Work. Fox, Marcia R. New York, W.W. Norton & Company, 1979.

Resume Writing Made Easy: A Practical Guide for Job Seekers. Coxford, Lola. Gorsuch Scarisbrick, Indiana, 1982.*

Resource Directory of Education and Training Opportunities and Other Services. Gray, Sandra T. Washington, D.C., Independent Sector, 1985.

Second Chance. Livesay, Herbert.*

"Sources of Job Satisfaction Among Service Volunteers." Gildron, Benjamin. *Journal of Voluntary Action Research 12,* No. 1 (1983).

Stop Out: Working Ways to Learn. Descriptions of nonpaid internships in government.*

"Stretching the Career Ladder." Foote, Joseph. *Foundation News,* pp. 24-28, January/February 1985.

The American Almanac of Jobs and Salaries. Wright, John W. New York, Avon Books, 1984.

The Career Game. Moore, Charles G., Ph.D. Ballantine Books.*

The Corporate Steeplechase, Predictable Crises in a Business Career. Blotnick, Srully. New York, Facts on File, 1984, p. 39.

The Encyclopedia of Second Careers. Hawes, Gene R. New York, Facts on File Publications, 1984.

The Job Search Companion; The Organizer for Job Seekers. Wallach, Ellen J. and Arnold, Peter. Boston, Massachusetts. The Harvard Common Press, 1984.

The Job Sharing Handbook. Olmstead, Barney, and Smith, Suzzane. Ten Speed Press, Berkeley, California, 1983.

The Nonprofit Board Book. Independent Community Consultants. West Memphis, Arkansas, 1983.*

The Seasons of a Man's Life. Levinson, Daniel J. New York, Ballantine Books, 1978, pg. 97ff.

The Three Boxes of Life and How To Get Out of Them; An Introduction to Life/Work Planning. Bolles, Richard R., Berkeley, California, Ten Speed Press, 1978.

The Time Trap; Managing Your Way Out. Mackenzie, Alec R. New York, New York, AMACOM, 1972.

"Types of Voluntary Action: A Definitional Essay." Smith, David Horton, et al. In *Voluntary Action Research,* 1972. Lexington, Massachusetts, Lexington Books, 1972.

Volunteers from the Workplace. Allen, Kerry Kenn; Chapin, Isolde; Keller, Shirley; and Hill, Donna. Washington, D.C., National Center for Voluntary Action, 1979.

What Color is Your Parachute? A Practical Manual for Job Hunters and Career Changers. Bolles, Richard N. Berkeley, California, Ten Speed Press.

Who's Hiring Who? Lathrop, Richard. Ten Speed Press, Berkeley, California.*

Why Should I Hire You? Thompson, Melvin R. Venture Press, 1975.

Women's Guide to Management Positions. Rogalin, Wilma C. and Pell, Arthur.*

Working in Foundations: Career Patterns of Women and Men. Odendahl, Teresa; Boris, Elizabeth; Daniels, Arlene. New York, The Foundation Center, 1985.

Appendix G

A DIRECTORY OF NONPROFIT "UMBRELLA" ORGANIZATIONS

The list below contains organizations (with their addresses) that serve as the umbrella organizations for cause-related nonprofits. This brief, and sampler, directory is divided into subject segments. Many of these organizations are excellent resources for career, educational, and other information.

Arts and Culture

American Association of Museums
1055 Thomas Jefferson Street, NW
Washington, DC 20036

American Council for the Arts
570 Seventh Avenue
New York, NY 10018

American Symphony Orchestra League
633 E Street, NW
Washington, DC 20004

Business Committee for the Arts
1775 Broadway
New York, NY 10010

Education

American Association of Colleges
1818 R Street, NW
Washington, DC 20009

American Association of University Women
2401 Virginia Avenue, NW
Washington, DC 20037

American Council on Education
1 Dupont Circle, NW
Washington, DC 20036

Council for the Advancement and Support of Education
11 Dupont Circle, NW
Washington, DC 20036

Council for Financial Aid to Education
650 Fifth Avenue
New York, NY 10019

Independent College Funds of America
420 Lexington Avenue
New York, NY 10017

National Associations of Independent
Colleges and Universities
1717 Massachusetts Avenue, NW
Washington, DC 20036

National Association of Independent Schools, Inc.
38 Tremont Street
Boston, MA 02109

National Catholic Educational Association
1 Dupont Circle, NW
Washington, DC 20036

Health/Mental Health

American Hospital Association
840 North Lake Shore Drive
Chicago, IL 60611

National Association for Hospital Development
8300 Greensboro Drive
McLean, VA 22102

National Health Council
70 West 40 Street
New York, NY 10018

Religion

Church Women United
777 UN Plaza
New York, NY 10117

Council of Jewish Federations
575 Lexington Avenue
New York, NY 10022

Federation of Protestant Welfare Agencies
281 Park Avenue South
New York, NY 10010

Leadership Conference of Women Religious (LCWR)
8808 Cameron Street
Silver Spring, MD 20910

National Catholic Development Conference
26 Front Street
Hempstead, NY 11150

National Council of Churches
475 Riverside Drive
New York, NY 10027

United States Catholic Conference
1312 Massachusetts Avenue, NW
Washington, DC 20036

Social Services

National Assembly of National Voluntary Health
and Social Welfare Organizations, Inc.
1346 Connecticut Avenue, NW
Washington, DC 20036

International

United Nations
United Nations Plaza
New York, NY 10017

UNESCO
c/o of United Nations, above

National Sector-wide Organizations

Institute on Nonprofit Organization Management
518 17th Street, #388
Denver, CO 80202

National Center for Charitable Statistics
1828 L Street, NW
Washington, DC 20036

National Charities Information Bureau
19 Union Square West
New York, NY 10003

National Society of Fund Raising Executives
1101 King Street, Suite 300
Arlington, VA 22314

Program on Nonprofit Organizations
Yale University
New Haven, CT 06520

The Council on Foundations
1828 L Street, NW
Washington, DC 20036

The Independent Sector
1828 L Street, NW
Washington, DC 20036

The United Way of America
United Way Plaza
Alexandria, VA 22314

The Urban Institute
2100 M Street, NW
Washington, DC 20037

Appendix H

A FORMAT FOR YOUR JOB SEARCH RESOURCE BINDER

This appendix suggests a format or structure for a three-ring binder or some other form of written-material holding device (let's hear it for those wonderful stationery stores) which would contain a number of sections to which you can add and delete material. The sections might include, for example:

SECTION 1—GOALS/OBJECTIVES

A one-page memo, carefully written by you, which contains a few listed job objectives in single sentence format, for example:

- to manage a first class health care delivery team in a major children's hospital
- to provide direct home visitation services to the frail elderly

followed by a few carefully written paragraphs expanding on your interests. The key phrases can be used in both letters and your interviews. This memo also will be a fast reminder of where you are heading if you ever get rattled or "lose your way" for a few days in the search.

SECTION 2—NOTES FOR TODAY'S NONPROFIT ORGANIZATION

Here you will keep notes you have prepared about the specific nonprofit organization you are going to visit today. Perhaps a copy of their annual report, program description, or fund-raising brochure. You may wish to insert a little pouch-like holder into the binder to hold such material. You may also have photocopied a copy of the Internal Revenue Service Form 990 on this NPO or your state's charitable organization registration material. Perhaps most important will be any notes you may have made on information you have gathered by talking to people familiar with the organization.

SECTION 3—YOUR RESUME

Multiple copies will be here, to be handed out at the first opportunity. Don't forget to keep extra copies with you so you can capitalize on those chance meetings.

SECTION 4—PERSONAL FACT SHEET

Insert a copy of your personal fact sheet, which will contain a very carefully prepared employment and salary history, references, and other data you might need to answer more detailed questions or complete application forms. See chapter 5 for more information. You might also put copies of any application forms you have already completed into this section so you can build on good phrases or add to your master application form as time goes by.

SECTION 5—A "BRAG" SHEET

Here you should force yourself to list, using action verbs, your key accomplishments from each position you have held. If this is your first paying job, do the same for school, homemaking, volunteer work, or whatever other activities you have been engaged in over the past few years. Push for quantifiable, solid results—you had some, no matter how you feel about your past work.

You will refer to this list (and add to it) as you go along, fine-tuning the descriptions and adding accomplishments you had forgotten. Glance over it after interviews since you may have brought out some important accomplishments or skills during an interview which you can now add.

SECTION 6—YOUR CALENDAR

This is a chronological display of the key actions you have planned out in your job search program or campaign. (See Action Step 18 in chapter 5 for more explicit suggestions on this.)

SECTION 7—YOUR CONTACTS

You need either a 3 x 5 pack of lined cards, a small address book used just for this purpose, or some other means of keeping track of who you see. It will be helpful to review these contacts occasionally with particularly helpful and knowledgeable persons in order to identify additional referrals and/or potential introductions they might mean for you.

SECTION 8—YOUR POTENTIAL JOB LIST

This will be a list of places you have contacted, researched, or heard about explicitly or in rumors. It will be revised and marked up constantly. Review it frequently and update and record comments about each potential position or nonprofit organization you hear about. It is easy to lose track of one "long shot" opportunity. Be rigorous. Be methodical. Try to stay organized! It will pay off!

SECTION 9—A SAMPLE LIST OF QUESTIONS FOR JOB INTERVIEWS

Put these in a simple format with enough room for answers to be jotted down after each question so that the data will be accurately and fully recorded. Be sure to leave room for extra questions and that critical spontaneous follow-up which only you can provide. Use a fresh set for each interview. Photocopy a supply in advance and keep the "master" copy clean so you can copy some more for additional interviews later.

If you feel comfortable with it, you can take this Job Search Resource Binder right into the interview. It can be very handy . . . and reassuring.

In addition, you should use a question-and-answer format for the tough questions you could be asked where you could use a little preplanning on the general thrust of your answer. *Do* plan ahead for these but *don't* try to develop a verbatim answer; the questions are a little different each time. Plan ahead and rehearse a little and you'll do fine!

Appendix I

SAMPLE INTERVIEW THANK YOU LETTER

Date

Ms./Mr._____
Director of Personnel
Community Service Society
120 Park Avenue South
New York, New York 10016

Dear Ms./Mr._____

Thank you for taking the time to speak with me on Tuesday, July 23, 1985 regarding the position of Executive Secretary. I enjoyed meeting you and learning more about the position and your organization.

As we discussed, I am familiar with nearly all of the tasks you identified. My background and work experience have prepared me to understand and carry out efficiently complex work projects. My personality makes this work possible in a cheerful, pleasant yet business-like manner. (Tailor this section directly to the specific position for which you interviewed.)

I am a good team player but also capable of self-starting and working on my own with minimal supervision.

I look forward to exploring this position and my qualifications to fill it with you further.

Sincerely yours,

TERRY W. MCADAM

Appendix J

CRITIQUE OF MY JOB SEARCH PERFORMANCE

To: (Your name)
From: Myself
Subject: Job Search Evaluation

This memorandum is to critique your recent job search and outline several important improvement opportunities upon which you might capitalize the next time you need to search for a new job.

Overall, you conducted a reasonably effective and efficient search. However, there are several areas which could be improved. Next time you should:

1. Remember to do something every day.
2. Follow more carefully the advice in Terry McAdam's book, *Careers in the Nonprofit Sector: Doing Well by Doing Good.*
3. Then, as appropriate, you will want to consider treating topics such as:

   - Clarity of your job objectives
   - Honesty of your preferences regarding geographic, other location, work style, nature of the surroundings, job characteristics
   - Thoroughness and readability of your search notes and files (can you read them easily now?)
   - Extent to which you established a network of contacts and used them
   - Completeness of your thank yous and follow-ups (it's not too late to fill in a few if you act quickly)
   - Recommendations on key process actions which could be strengthened
   - Thoroughness of your assessment of all aspects of your job offer

The key to this critique is to focus it on concrete actions you should be able to take next time you consider changing jobs. It isn't easy to have the discipline to write this critique, but it will save you much pain the next time around. Please do it for your own sake!

Appendix K

SELECTED GLOSSARY OF NONPROFIT TERMINOLOGY

A number of sources were consulted to compile this brief glossary. They include the staff and resources of The Taft Group, Washington, D.C.; *How To Hire the Right Fund-Raising Consultant*, by Arthur D. Raybin (Washington, D.C.: The Taft Group, 1985); *The Foundation Directory*, tenth edition, Loren Renz, editor (New York: The Foundation Center, 1985), and *Corporate Philanthropy*, (Washington, D.C., The Council on Foundations, 1982).

AAFRC. American Association of Fund-Raising Counsel, Inc., the New York-based organization to which 31 of the major consulting firms in the field belong.

ANNUAL CAMPAIGN. See ANNUAL FUND DRIVE.

ANNUAL FUND DRIVE. An effort to solicit contributions on a yearly cycle to cover a gift-supported institution's operating expenses (the difference between income and expenses). Also known as a BUDGET or MAINTENANCE DRIVE, and in churches as an EVERY-MEMBER CANVASS.

ANNUAL GIVING. Contributions made in response to the annual fund drive.

ANNUAL REPORT. A voluntary report issued by a foundation or corporate-giving program which provides financial data and descriptions of grant-making activities; reports vary in format from simple typewritten documents to detailed, four-color publications which provide substantial information about the grant-making program. A current listing of publications issued by corporate grantmakers is provided in the latest edition of Taft's *Corporate Giving Yellow Pages.*

ASSETS. The amount of money, stocks, bonds, real estate, or other holdings of an organization, often invested, and the income earned from investment used to make grants or provide operating income.

BENEFICIARY. In philanthropy, an individual or organization which receives the contributed funds. Also known as the donee or grantee.

BOARD. As in "the board," refers to the board of trustees of a gift-supported institution or organization. See also TRUSTEE.

BRICKS AND MORTAR. Informal term for buildings or construction project grants; see also CAPITAL GRANT.

BUDGET DRIVE. See ANNUAL FUND DRIVE.

CAMPAIGN. Any type of fund-raising effort that involves solicitation of direct contributions to achieve a monetary goal, as opposed to a special event which raises funds by such means as raffles, sale of a table at a benefit dinner, and so on.

CAMPAIGN PLAN. A comprehensive schedule, budget, and strategy statement prepared at the outset of a major fund-raising drive.

CAPITAL CAMPAIGN. Usually a three- to five-year program in which pledges, payable over that time period, are sought for such objectives as construction projects, renovations, and endowments.

CAPITAL GRANT. Grant to provide funding for buildings, construction, or equipment, rather than program or operating expenses; see also BRICKS AND MORTAR. Also known as CAPITAL SUPPORT.

CASE. See CASE STATEMENT.

CASE STATEMENT. The long-range plan for a gift-supported organization, presented in a fund-raising context, that sets forth, in generally no more than twelve to fifteen pages, the organization's history, where it stands now, its plans for the future, the difference that contributed funds will make in realizing those plans, and how the funds will be obtained.

CHALLENGE GRANT. A grant award that is paid only if the beneficiary is able to raise additional funds from other source(s); often used to stimulate giving from other foundations or donors. See also EMPLOYEE MATCHING GIFT, MATCHING GRANT.

COMMUNITY FOUNDATION. A publicly supported organization which makes grants for social, educational, religious, or other charitable purposes in a specific community or region. Funds are usually retained in an endowment; the income earned is then used to make grants. Some community foundations are designated by the IRS as private foundations, but most are classified as PUBLIC CHARITY eligible for the maximum tax-deductible contributions from the public. See also FOUNDATION.

COMMUNITY FUND. An organized community program which makes annual appeals to the general public for funds, usually not retained in an endowment but used for operational support of local social and health service agencies. See also FEDE-RATED GIVING PROGRAM.

CONSULTANT. In the fund-raising context, an individual (or a firm) who applies proven fund-raising research methodology and management principles to assist and guide a gift-supported organization in achieving its fund-raising objectives without actually soliciting contributions. A consultant provides either RESIDENT DIRECTION or continuing counseling with frequent site visits. Also known as COUNSEL.

COOPERATIVE VENTURE. A joint contributory effort between two or more grantmakers (including foundations, corporations, and government agencies). Partners may share in funding responsibilities or contribute information and technical resources. See also JOINT VENTURE.

CORPORATE CONTRIBUTIONS. A broad term encompassing all of a corporation's charitable contributions whether they are made through a company- sponsored foundation or a direct giving program, whether they are cash or in-kind.

CORPORATE FOUNDATION. Also known as company-sponsored foundation, a foundation whose funds are derived from a profit-making corporation or company and whose primary purpose is the making of grants; usually it is an independent organization with its own endowment and is subject to the same rules and regulations as other private foundations. See also FOUNDATION.

COUNSEL. See CONSULTANT.

DECLINING GRANT. A multi-year grant which grows smaller each year in the expectation that the donee organization will raise other funds to make up the gap.

DEFERRED GIVING. See PLANNED GIVING.

DEVELOPMENT. The art of cultivating prospective donors and obtaining their support; the term is often used to describe the fund-raising staff function within a gift-supported institution.

DIRECT GIVING. Contributions made directly from corporate revenues rather than indirectly through a foundation or charitable trust.

DISTRIBUTION COMMITTEE. The committee responsible for making grant decisions.

DONEE. The individual or organization which receives a grant; also known as the grantee.

DONOR. The source of a contribution (gift or pledge) or grant; may be an individual, corporation, or foundation; also known as the grantor.

EMPLOYEE MATCHING GIFT. A contribution to a charitable organization by an individual which is matched by a similar contribution from his or her employer.

ENDOWMENT. Funds intended to be kept permanently and invested to provide income for continued support.

ENDOWMENT CAMPAIGN. A capital campaign with focus on raising endowment— funds that will be invested to produce yearly income for operating expenses.

EVERY-MEMBER CANVASS. See ANNUAL FUND DRIVE.

EXECUTIVE SEARCH. Usually involves using the services of a consultant who specializes in finding executive-level staff, most often the head development officer but also others such as a finance officer, database administrator, or proposal writer.

FAMILY FOUNDATION. A foundation whose funds and assets are derived from a single family. Often family members serve as officers or board members of the foundation and play an influential role in the foundation's affairs. See also FOUNDATION.

FEASIBILITY STUDY. See PRECAMPAIGN STUDY.

FEDERATED GIVING PROGRAM. A joint fund-raising effort usually administered by a nonprofit "umbrella" organization which in turn distributes contributed funds to several nonprofit agencies. United Way and similar funds, and joint arts councils are examples. See also COMMUNITY FUND.

FINANCIAL REPORT. A report detailing how grant or other funds were used by an organization. Many donors or grantsmakers require this kind of report from grantees.

FISCAL AGENT. A tax-exempt (501(c)(3)) entity that acts as sponsor for an organization that does not have tax-exempt status.

FORM 990-PF. The annual information return that all private foundations must submit to the Internal Revenue Service; a similar form may also be filed with the appropriate state offices.

FOUNDATION. Often but not always, a grant-making organization. Various types of foundations exist. See also COMMUNITY, CORPORATE, FAMILY, GENERAL PURPOSE, OPERATING, and SPECIAL PURPOSE FOUNDATIONS.

FUNGIBLE. Legal term designating movable goods, any part of which can replace another part, as in money used to discharge a debt. In fund-raising, used to describe a situation, for example, in which donors to a school prefer to contribute toward scholarship aid, thus creating a campaign shortfall in funds for faculty compensation. The institution needs less from its operating budget and transferred to provide for scholarships and money is freed within this budget for increased faculty compensation.

GENERAL PURPOSE FOUNDATION. A foundation which awards grants in many different fields of interest. See also SPECIAL PURPOSE FOUNDATION.

GIFT. An outright contribution of money, securities, or other property. Also, a payment toward a multi-year pledge. See also PLEDGE.

GIFT-SUPPORTED INSTITUTION. Contemporary term for a nonprofit, tax-exempt organization. Donors to it are able to deduct contributions from their income tax returns as charitable contributions. Often called (501)(c)(3) organizations, referring to their designation in the tax code. See also NONPROFIT, PUBLIC CHARITY.

GRANT. A contribution of money to an organization, institution, group, or individual, usually but not always to accomplish a specific purpose.

GRASSROOTS FUND-RAISING. Efforts to raise money from local community individuals or groups, and generally includes such activities as bake sales, auctions, benefits, dances, and a range of other activities.

IN-KIND CONTRIBUTION A contribution in lieu of money, such as of equipment, supplies, or other property.

INTERNAL AUDIT. Consultant's review of an institution's fund-raising staff and procedures to assess the organization's readiness for a major campaign. See also PRE-CAMPAIGN STUDY.

JOINT VENTURE. Many nonprofits are able to create profit-driven operations so long as the income derived does not exceed a certain percentage. Arrangements with for-profit, commercial businesses to set up and jointly run such operations are referred to as joint ventures.

LEVERAGE. Leverage occurs when an amount of money is given with the express purpose of attracting larger gifts from other sources or of providing the organization with the tools it needs to raise other kinds of funds.

LOANED EXECUTIVE. An employee (usually management-level) who is granted temporary, paid leave from his or her corporate duties to serve in some capacity (usually related to his or her job skills) with a nonprofit organization.

MAINTENANCE DRIVE. See ANNUAL FUND DRIVE.

MATCHING GRANT. A grant which is made to match funds provided by another donor; see also CHALLENGE GRANT, EMPLOYEE MATCHING GIFT.

NONPROFIT. A term describing the Internal Revenue Service's designation of an organization whose income is not used for the benefit or private gain of stockholders, directors, or any other persons with an interest in the company.

NSFRE. National Society of Fund Raising Executives, a Washington-based organization to which more than 6,000 development officers or fund-raisers belong.

NUCLEUS FUND. A "kitty" established at the outset of a campaign, usually limited to board members who make early gifts at levels that serve as examples for others.

OPERATING FOUNDATION. A fund or endowment designated by the Internal Revenue Service as a private foundation whose primary purpose is to conduct research, social welfare, or other programs determined by its governing body or establishment charter. See also FOUNDATION.

PILOT PROJECT GRANT. A grant to fund a first-of-its-kind program in one place to determine how well it works and if it might be replicated elsewhere. See also SEED MONEY.

PLANNED GIVING. Contributions generally not transferred immediately to a gift-supported institution, such as gifts made by bequest, life insurance beneficiary clauses, and more complex gifts that, in exchange for the contribution, return to the donors or their heirs an interest in or income from the gift for a specified time.

PLANNING GRANT. Grant that funds the planning processes of a program.

PLEDGE. A commitment to make a contribution that will be paid over a period of time, usually three years.

PRECAMPAIGN STUDY. The first phase of a CAMPAIGN, consisting of two parts: feasibility tests to determine if the preliminary goals can be achieved, and the internal audit to evaluate the organization's capabilities for a successful campaign.

PROGRAM OFFICER. A staff member who on the grant-giving side reviews grant proposals and processes applications for the board of trustees; on the grant-seeking side, the program officer might be responsible for developing, seeking funds for, and carrying out the program.

PROPOSAL. A written application submitted to a foundation in requesting a grant, often supplied with supporting documents.

PROSPECT RESEARCH. A systematic approach assessing prospective donors' interests and abilities to contribute.

PUBLIC CHARITY. An organization designated as tax-exempt under Section 501(c)(3) of the Internal Revenue Service Code, which derives at least one-third of its funding from the general public and which maintains or aids social, educational, religious, or other charitable activities. Public charities engage in grant-making, direct service, or other tax-exempt activities. See also GIFT-SPONSORED INSTITUTION, NONPROFIT.

QUERY LETTER. Also known as letter of inquiry. A brief letter outlining an organization's activities and its request for funding, sent to foundations to determine whether it would be appropriate to submit a full grant proposal.

RECONNAISSANCE STUDY. A short study by a consultant, encompassing confidential interviews with volunteer leaders (see also VOLUNTEER) and prospective donors to assess a campaign's progress at mid-point and to determine if adjustments are required. Also known as a SECOND STUDY.

RESIDENT DIRECTION. Refers to the coordination and overall management of a campaign by an on-site consultant.

RESTRICTED GRANT. A grant to be used for defined purposes or within a certain time, determined by the grantmaker.

RFP. Request for Proposal; for example, when the government issues a new contract or grant program, it typically sends out RFPs to agencies that might be qualified to participate.

SECOND STUDY. See RECONNAISSANCE STUDY.

SEED MONEY. An initial grant or contribution given to start a new project or organization. See also PILOT PROJECT GRANT.

SOCIAL AUDIT. An examination of a corporation's actions and use of resources as they affect both employees and the communities and society in which it operates.

SOLICITOR. One, usually a volunteer, who asks others to support an institution or a case. See also VOLUNTEER.

SPECIAL PURPOSE FOUNDATION. A foundation which focuses its grant-making activities in one or a few special areas of interest. See also FOUNDATION.

STEERING COMMITTEE. The leadership group, usually including a number of key board members, responsible for both the policy-setting and major solicitations in a fundraising program; steering committees may also be formed to develop new service programs during their start-up phase.

TELEMARKETING. Also known as telefundraising. The efficient, organized, and cost-effective method for reaching donors or clients in an effort to increase giving or sales. Ordinarily, paid telephone callers solicit support after a series of letters has been used to explain the case statement to potential donors.

TRUSTEE. A member of a governing board. May also be referred to as "directors." See also BOARD.

VOLUNTEER. One who gives time freely in support of an institution or a cause. They are crucial in any fund-raising program.

Appendix L

COMPENSATION ANALYSIS WORKSHEET

The following items should be considered in analyzing a compensation package offer. Keep in mind that each NPO may provide its employees with only a modest number of the items on the list below. The utility of putting it altogether is that you can:

- Compare the offer to your current situation, and
- Look at the possibility of negotiating trade-offs of one benefit for another.

Your analysis should cover the items listed on the following pages.

ITEM	Current Situation	The Offer	Difference	Comments
Direct Compensation				
Basic Salary				
Bonus Possibilities				
Expense Allowance				
Transportation Allowance				
Parking allowance/subsidy				
Housing Allowance				
Matching Savings Plan				
Voluntary Salary Deduction				
Pension Plan				
(Pension vesting in years)				
Deferred Compensation				
Severance Pay				
Support for Academic Training				
Leave				
Vacation (in weeks)				
Sick leave (in weeks)				
Compensatory time				
Release time for Consulting/Teaching				

Health Benefits
Group Life Insurance
Group Hospital Insurance
Accidental Death and Disability Insurance
Major Medical Insurance
Catastrophic Incident Health Insurance
Dental Insurance
Eye Care
Direct Disability Pay
Annual Physical Exam

Other Benefits
Paid Memberships (professional)
Paid Memberships (health/social/recreational)
Legal Assistance
Financial Planning Assistance
Tax Planning Assistance
Accounting Assistance
Mortgage Access/Assistance
Credit Union
Short-Term Loans
Retirement Planning Assistance
Free Services for Family Members
Termination notice in advance

BUILD YOUR FUND-RAISING LIBRARY WITH TAFT'S FUND-RAISING STRATEGY RESOURCES

CORPORATE GIVING WATCH - monthly newsletter
With corporate giving now clearly the fastest growing segment of philanthropy, the successful development director seeking corporate funds needs plenty of useful intelligence on the corporate giving scene—on the individual companies, their executives, and their giving. *Corporate Giving Watch* is the *only* newsletter designed expressly to deliver all this crucial information—and in a comprehensive yet concise format.

CORPORATE PHILANTHROPY IN AMERICA: New Perspectives for the Eighties
This Taft Special Report analyzes corporate giving in this decade, telling you *the* nine reasons corporations give, where the money goes by industry and by area of activity, and what the future holds in terms of trends, increases, or decreases. Bibliography and tables included make this an invaluable resource for updating your fund-raising plans and strategies.

FOUNDATION GIVING WATCH - monthly newsletter
It's a fact of life in fund raising that most foundations do not do a very good job of informing the public about their activities. You can be sure that decisions are being made all the time which affect your chances of getting foundation grants. *That's why you need Foundation Giving Watch*—a monthly newsletter devoted to telling you the news about foundations and, most important, what it means to you.

HOW TO HIRE THE RIGHT FUND-RAISING CONSULTANT: Getting the Most from Your Campaign
From precampaign planning through a campaign's final phases, this book shares the tips and secrets of planning, interviewing, negotiating, and working with a fund-raising consultant to create that often elusive chemistry needed for a successful campaign. Presents how-to techniques and checklists punctuated with illustrative anecdotes; also includes sample letters, agendas, agreement form, schedules, glossary.

HOW TO RATE YOUR DEVELOPMENT OFFICE: A Fund-Raising Primer for the Chief Executive
Outstanding guide covering every detail needed to clarify and assess the success of your development office. Superb manual for every chief executive—whether you're planning to institute a new development program or looking to make your current fund-raising office more productive.

PRIVATE FUNDING ADVISOR - monthly newsletter
The premier monthly newsletter designed to tell you how to supplement your government funding. Publicly supported organizations can raise funds in the private sector, and this newsletter will tell you how and where to do it.

TAFT'S FIVE-STAR FUND-RAISING PACKAGE

UP YOUR ACCOUNTABILITY: How to Up Your Funding Credibility by Upping Your Accounting Ability
The first, nontechnical, accounting "textbook" ever written specifically to meet the needs of the nonprofit manager or student. Gives you the basic information you need to understand the financial working of a nonprofit group and to do realistic financial planning.

THE 13 MOST COMMON FUND-RAISING MISTAKES AND HOW AVOID THEM
This down-to-earth, witty, cartoon-illustrated book shows how adherence to a few basic principles can yield more grants, more gifts, more wills and bequests. Written by Paul H. Schneiter and Donald T. Nelson, it draws on exceptional experience in legendary Mormon fund-raising circles.

BUILDING A BETTER BOARD: A Guide to Effective Leadership
For every board member or nonprofit executive interacting with trustees, this succinct booklet will help you gain maximum board effectiveness through understanding the roles and expectations of each and every board member. Written by Andrew Swanson who brings over 25 years of practical working experience as president or trustee on more than 30 nonprofit boards. Available for quantity purchase.

THE PROPOSAL WRITER'S SWIPE FILE: 15 Winning Fund-Raising Proposals
The grants-oriented fund raiser's "best friend" in helping design successful applications. Pattern your proposals on these examples of actual winning proposals.

PROSPECTING: Searching out the Philanthropic Dollar
The most comprehensive functional manual on donor research available today, covering every major aspect of prospect research. Includes valuable Forms Kit enabling you to conveniently record your prospecting research.

The above five valuable learning tools may be purchased for one special price.

See order form on back for more of Taft's fund-raising resources.

BUILD YOUR FUND-RAISING LIBRARY WITH TAFT'S CAREER/MANAGEMENT RESOURCES

CAREER DEVELOPMENT

CAREERS IN THE NONPROFIT SECTOR: Doing Well by Doing Good

How do you make it to the top (or get your foot in the door) of this $150 billion industry? This book explodes many a myth about the third sector as it explores job opportunities, competition, and trends from job search to interview to future prospects. Includes interviews with top nonprofit professionals, a listing of top nonprofits, worksheets, and job hunting checklists.

CONFESSIONS OF A FUND RAISER: Lessons of an Instructive Career

A heartwarming, uplifting, funny, candid, and revealing memoir from Maurice G. Gurin, the "elder statesman of the fund-raising profession." Chronicles his remarkable career as fund-raising consultant to some of America's most well-known philanthropists and institutions.

THE NONPROFIT EXECUTIVE - monthly newsletter

Action-oriented monthly newsletter for nonprofit managers. The first newsletter dedicated to advancing the careers of executive-level nonprofit managers and development officers. Your way of keeping in touch with all the trends, new development ideas, events, how-to techniques, and concepts that affect your performance and success. Features a special careers/jobs section.

NONPROFIT MANAGEMENT

DEAR CHRIS: Letters to a Volunteer Fund Raiser

John Verdery's 40 years as successful fund raiser and board member make these 16 inspirational and educational letters the perfect tool to help build a core of committed, confident, and articulate volunteer solicitors. Indispensable for the campaign volunteer, it is also ideal for board members, ceo's professional staff, and development directors. Available for quantity purchase.

DO OR DIE: Survival for Nonprofits

For the nonprofit executive who recognizes the advantage of "profit thinking for nonprofit organizations." Insightful exploration of nonprofit management approaches—separates myth from fact.

MANAGING CONTRIBUTED FUNDS AND ASSETS: The Tax-Exempt Financial Planning Manual

By means of an ingenious system of actual ledger worksheets and explanatory text, the author takes you through the accounting and financial planning steps needed to maximize cash, increase yields, and build endowment. More than just a manual system, the application of the information and techniques presented will also improve reporting practices and procedures within your organization. Purchase includes blank ledger worksheets for your use.

See order form on back for more of Taft's fund-raising resources.

Qty.	Publication	Price	P&H
I. FUND-RAISING STRATEGY			
____	☐ Corporate Giving Watch/Giving Profiles (newsletter)	$127.00	0.00
____	☐ Corporate Philanthropy in America	$27.00	$2.25
____	☐ Foundation Giving Watch/Foundation Updates (newsletter) One year, 12 issues. Regular price $127.00—save $30.00 .	$97.00	$0.00
____	☐ How to Hire the Right Fund-Raising Consultant . . .	$24.95	$3.00
____	☐ How to Rate Your Development Office	$21.95	$3.00
____	☐ Introduction to Planning Giving	$24.95	$5.00
____	☐ Private Funding Advisor (newsletter) One year, 12 issues. Regular price $117.00—save $30.00	$87.00	$0.00
____	☐ Prospecting: Searching Out the Philanthropic Dollar .	$23.95	$2.25
____	☐ Taft's Five-Star Fund-Raising Package	$75.95	$10.00
____	☐ The Proposal Writer's Swipe File	$18.95	$2.25
____	☐ The Thirteen Most Common Fund-Raising Mistakes .	$17.95	$2.25
____	☐ There's Plenty of Money for Nonprofits Willing to Earn Their Share Circle your choice: hardbound or 3-ring .	$57.00	$3.00
II. MARKETING STRATEGY			
____	☐ The Complete Taft Marketing Strategy Library Full price $203.95—save $18.95	$185.00	$30.00
____	☐ Dear Friend: Mastering the Art of Direct Mail Fund Raising	$47.50	$5.00
____	☐ Do or Die: Survival for Nonprofits	$13.95	$2.25
____	☐ The Complete Guide to Money-Making Ventures for Nonprofit Organizations	$47.50	$10.00
____	☐ Philanthropy and Marketing: New Strategies for Fund Raising	$47.50	$10.00
____	☐ Telepledge: The Complete Guide to Mail-Phone Fund Raising	$47.50	$10.00
III. DONOR RESEARCH			
____	☐ The Complete Taft Donor Research Library Basic II System and other books below Full price $1,176.00—save $150.00	$1,026.00	$50.00
____	☐ Taft Basic II System—1987 (includes Taft Corporate Information System and Taft Foundation Information System) Full price $774.00—save $147.00	$627.00	$25.00
____	☐ Taft Corporate Information System—1987 (includes Taft Corporate Giving Directory and Corporate Giving Watch/Corporate Giving Profiles Full price $424.00—save $27.00	$397.00	$15.00
____	☐ Taft Foundation Information System—1987 (includes Taft Foundation Reporter and Foundation Giving Watch/Foundation Updates) Full price $424.00—save $47.00	$377.00	$15.00
____	☐ America's Hidden Philanthropic Wealth: Tomorrow's Potential Foundation Giants Individual report (comes w/1 binder)	$79.95	$10.00
	1-year series subscription (4 issues) (comes w/2 binders) .	$227.00	$15.00
____	☐ America's Wealthiest People: Their Philanthropic and Nonprofit Affiliations . .	$57.50	$5.00
____	☐ Corporate Giving Yellow Pages	$67.50	$5.00
____	☐ People in Philanthropy 1986-87 edition	$197.00	$10.00

Qty.	Publication	Price	P&H
____	☐ Taft Corporate Giving Directory (1987 edition) . . .	$297.00	$15.0
____	☐ Taft Foundation Reporter (1987 edition)	$297.00	$15.0
IV. NONPROFIT MANAGEMENT			
____	☐ The Complete Taft Management Library Full price $381.35—save $37.35	$344.00	$25.0
____	☐ Beyond Profit: The Complete Guide to Managing the Nonprofit Organization	$18.95	$3.0
____	☐ Building a Better Board: A Guide to Effective Leadership		
	1 to 4 copies—each at	$9.50	$2.7
	5 to 9 copies—each at	$8.50	$5.?
	10 or more copies—each at	$7.50	$10.0
____	☐ Dear Chris: Letters to a Volunteer Fund Raiser		
	1 to 4 copies—each at	$24.95	$3.0
	5 to 9 copies—each at	$21.95	$7.0
	10 or more copies—each at	$18.95	$15.0
____	☐ Managing Contributed Funds & Assets: The Tax-Exempt Financial Planning Manual	$167.00	$10.0
____	☐ The President and Board of Directors	$145.00	$10.0
____	☐ Up Your Accountability	$15.95	$2.?
V. NONPROFIT CAREER DEVELOPMENT			
____	☐ The Complete Taft Career Development Library Full price $141.90—save $14.90	$127.00	$5.0
____	☐ Careers in the Nonprofit Sector: Doing Well by Doing Good	$24.95	$3.0
____	☐ Confessions of a Fund Raiser	$24.95	$3.0
____	☐ Nonprofit Executive (newsletter) One year, 12 issues .	$87.00	$0.0
VI. COMPUTER RESOURCES			
____	☐ The Complete Taft Computer Resources Library (includes books listed plus the TEAM SYSTEM Demo) Full price $186.45—save $19.45	$167.00	$20.0
____	☐ Basic Computer Knowledge for Nonprofits	$67.50	$10.0
____	☐ The Guide to Software For Nonprofits	$79.00	$10.0

TEAM SYSTEM Software

		Price	P&H
____	☐ TEAM SYSTEM Development Package	$1,350.00	$10.0
____	☐ TEAM SYSTEM Profile Master Module	$495.00	$7.5
____	☐ Special Demo Package	$39.95	$3.7

Please indicate your
• computer brand and model: _____
• installed RAM: _____K ● MS-DOS version # _____
• how many names you wish to store (appox.) _____
Check one: hard disk _____ or 2 floppies _____

☐ **SEND ME YOUR LATEST CATALOG.**

To order, please complete the information below and send to:

The Taft Group
5130 MacArthur Blvd., N.W.
Washington, D.C. 20016

To order by phone, call
800-424-3761
202-966-7086

Name _____

Title _____

Organization _____

Address _____

City/State/Zip _____

Signature _____
(Order cannot be processed without signature)

Telephone (_____) _____

All prices subject to change without prior notice. For purchases under $55. payment must accompany order.

Form of Payment:
☐ My check is enclosed. Taft pays postage and handling on prepaid order
☐ Bill me. P.O.# _____ (attach P.
☐ Please charge to my VISA/MasterCard

_____ expires _____ / _____
(credit card number)   mo   yr

Total Price of items ordered $ _____

Postage and Handling (P&H) $ _____

Total $ _____

Enclose payment and Taft pays your postage and handling
Please allow 4 to 6 weeks for delivery   S:7162